THE ISLANDS

THE ISLANDS

A. ALBERTS

PERIPLUS

Paperback edition published in 1999 by Periplus Editions (HK) Ltd.

ISBN 962-593-261-5
Printed in Singapore

Publisher: Eric Oey

Distributors

Asia Pacific   Berkeley Books Pte. Ltd.
                      5 Little Road, #08-01
                      Singapore 536983
                      Tel: (65) 280-1330
                      Fax: (65) 280-6290

Indonesia   PT Wira Mandala Pustaka,
                      (Java Books – Indonesia)
                      Jl. Kelapa Gading Kirana
                      Blok A14 No.17, Jakarta 14240
                      Tel: (62-21) 451-5351
                      Fax: (62-21) 453-4987

Japan   Tuttle Publishing
                      RK Building 2nd Floor
                      2-13-10 Shimo Meguro, Meguro-Ku
                      Tokyo 153 0064, Japan
                      Tel: (03) 5437-0171
                      Fax: (03) 5437-0755

United States   Tuttle Publishing
                      Distribution Center
                      Airport Industrial Park
                      364 Innovation Drive
                      North Clarendon, VT 05759-9436
                      Tel: (802) 773-8930, (800) 526-2778

Preparation and publication of this work were supported by the Translation and Publication Programs of the National Endowment for the Humanities, the Foundation for the Promotion of the Translation of Dutch Literary Works and the Prince Bernhard Fund, to whom acknowledgment is gratefully made.

Contents

Preface

THIS VOLUME is one of a series of literary works written by the Dutch about their lives in the former colony of the Dutch East Indies, now the Republic of Indonesia. This realm of more than three thousand islands is roughly one quarter the size of the continental United States. It consists of the four Greater Sunda Islands—Sumatra, larger than California; Java, about the size of New York State; Borneo, about the size of France (presently called Kalimantan); and Celebes, about the size of North Dakota (now called Sulawesi). East from Java is a string of smaller islands called the Lesser Sunda Islands, which includes Bali, Lombok, Sumba, Sumbawa, Flores, and Timor. Further east from the Lesser Sunda Islands lies New Guinea, now called Irian Barat, which is the second largest island in the world. Between New Guinea and Celebes there is a host of smaller islands, often known as the Moluccas, that includes a group once celebrated as the Spice Islands.

One of the most volcanic regions in the world, the Malay archipelago is tropical in climate and has a diverse population. Some 250 languages are spoken in Indonesia and it is remarkable that a population of such widely differing cultural and ethnic backgrounds adopted the Malay language as its *lingua franca* from about the fifteenth century, although that language was spoken at first only in parts of Sumatra and the Malay peninsula (now Malaysia).

Though the smallest of the Greater Sunda Islands, Java has always been the most densely populated, with about two-thirds of all Indonesians living there. In many ways a history of Indonesia is, first and foremost, the history of Java.

But in some ways Java's prominence is misleading because it belies the great diversity of this island realm. For instance, the destination of the first Europeans who sailed to Southeast Asia was not Java but the Moluccas. It was that "odiferous pistil" (as Motley called the clove), as well as nutmeg and mace, that drew the Portuguese to a group of small islands in the Ceram and Banda Seas in the early part of the sixteenth century. Pepper was another profitable commodity and attempts to obtain it brought the Portuguese into conflict with Atjeh, an Islamic sultanate in northern Sumatra, and with Javanese traders who, along with merchants from India, had been the traditional middlemen of the spice trade. The precedent of European intervention had been set, and was to continue for nearly four centuries.

Although subsequent history is complicated in its causes and effects, one may propose certain generalities. The Malay realm was essentially a littoral one. Even in Java, the interior was sparsely populated and virtually unknown to the foreign intruders coming from China, India, and Europe. Whoever ruled the seas controlled the archipelago, and for the next three centuries the key needed to unlock the riches of Indonesia was mastery of the Indian Ocean. The nations who thus succeeded were, in turn, Portugal, Holland, and England, and one can trace the shifting of power in the prominence and decline of their major cities in the Orient. Goa, Portugal's stronghold in India, gave way to Batavia in the Dutch East Indies, while Batavia was overshadowed by Singapore by the end of the nineteenth century. Although all three were relatively small nations, they were maritime giants. Their success was partly due to the internecine warfare between the countless city-states, principalities, and native autocrats. The Dutch were masters at playing one against the other.

Religion was a major factor in the fortunes of Indonesia. The Portuguese expansion was in part a result of Portugal's crusade against Islam, which was quite as ferocious and intransigent as the holy war of the Mohammedans. Islam may be considered a unifying force in the archipelago; it cut across all levels of society and provided a rallying point for resistance to foreign intrusion. Just as the Malay language had done linguistically, Islam proved to be a syncretizing force when there was no united front. One of the causes of Portugal's demise was its inflexible antagonism to Islam, and later the Dutch found resistance to their rule fueled by religious fervor as well as political dissatisfaction.

Holland ventured to reach the tropical antipodes not only because their nemesis, Philip II of Spain, annexed Portugal and forbade the Dutch entry to Lisbon. The United Netherlands was a nation of merchants, a brokerage house for northern Europe, and it wanted to get to the source of tropical wealth itself. Dutch navigators and traders knew the location of the fabled Indies, they were well acquainted with Portuguese achievements at sea, and counted among its members individuals who had worked for the Portuguese. Philip II simply accelerated a process that was inevitable.

At first, various individual enterprises outfitted ships and sent them to the Far East in a far from lucrative display of free enterprise. Nor was the first arrival of the Dutch in the archipelago auspicious, though it may have been symbolic of subsequent developments. In June 1596 a Dutch fleet of four ships anchored off the coast of Java. Senseless violence and a total disregard for local customs made the Dutch unwelcome on those shores.

During the seventeenth century the Dutch extended their influence in the archipelago by means of superior naval strength, use of armed intervention which was often ruthless, by shrewd politicking and exploitation of local differences. Their cause was helped by the lack of a cohesive force to withstand them. Yet the seventeenth century also saw a number of men who were eager to know the new realm, who investigated the language and the mores of the people they encountered, and who studied the flora and fauna. These were men who not only put the Indies on the map of trade routes, but who also charted riches of other than commercial value.

It soon became apparent to the Dutch that these separate ventures did little to promote welfare. In 1602 Johan van Oldenbarneveldt, the Advocate of the United Provinces, managed to negotiate a contract which in effect merged all these individual enterprises into one United East India Company, better known under its Dutch acronym as the VOC. The merger ensured a monopoly at home, and the Company set out to obtain a similar insurance in the Indies. This desire for exclusive rights to the production and marketing of spices and other commodities proved to be a double-edged sword.

The VOC succeeded because of its unrelenting naval vigilance in discouraging European competition, and because the Indies were a politically unstable region. And even though the Company was only interested in its balance sheet, it soon found itself burdened with an expanding empire and an indolent bureaucracy which, in the eighteenth century, became not only unwieldy but tolerant of graft and extortion. Furthermore, even though its profits were far below what they were rumored to be, the Company kept its dividends artificially high and was soon forced to borrow money to pay the interest on previous loans. When Holland's naval supremacy was seriously challenged by the British in 1780, a blockade kept the Company's ships from reaching Holland, and the discrepancy between capital and expenditures increased dramatically until the Company's deficit was so large it had to request state aid. In 1798, after nearly two centuries, the Company ceased to exist. Its debt of 140 million guilders was assumed by the state, and the commercial enterprise became a colonial empire.

At the beginning of the nineteenth century, Dutch influence was still determined by the littoral character of the region. Dutch presence in the archipelago can be said to have lasted three and a half centuries, but if one defines colonialism as the subjugation of an *entire* area, and dates it from the time when the last independent domain was conquered—in this case Atjeh in northern Sumatra—then the Dutch colonial empire lasted less than half a century. Effective government could only be claimed for the Moluccas, certain portions of Java (by no means the entire island), a southern portion of Celebes, and some coastal regions of Sumatra and Borneo. Yet it is also true that precisely because Indonesia was an insular realm, Holland never needed to muster a substantial army such as the one the British had to maintain in the large subcontinent of India. The extensive interiors of islands such as Sumatra, Borneo, or Celebes were not penetrated because, for the seaborne empire of commercial interests, exploration of such regions was unprofitable, hence not desirable.

The nature of Holland's involvement changed with the tenure of Herman Willem Daendels as Governor-General, just after the French revolution. Holland declared itself a democratic nation in

1795, allied itself with France—which meant a direct confrontation with England—and was practically a vassal state of France until 1810. Though reform, liberal programs, and the mandate of human rights were loudly proclaimed in Europe, they did not seem to apply to the Asian branch of the family of man. Daendels exemplified this double standard. He evinced reforms, either in fact or on paper, but did so in an imperious manner and with total disregard for native customs and law (known as *adat*). Stamford Raffles, who was the chief administrator of the British interim government from 1811 to 1816, expanded Daendels's innovations, which included tax reform and the introduction of the land-rent system, which was based on the assumption that all the land belonged to the colonial administration. By the time Holland regained its colonies in 1816, any resemblance to the erstwhile Company had vanished. In its place was a firmly established, paternalistic, colonial government which ruled by edict and regulation, supported a huge bureaucracy, and sought to make the colonies turn a profit as well as legislate its inhabitants' manner of living.

It is not surprising that for the remainder of the nineteenth century, a centralized authority instituted changes from above that were often in direct conflict with Javanese life and welfare. One such change, which was supposed to increase revenues and improve the life of the Javanese peasant, was the infamous "Cultivation System" *(Cultuurstelsel)*. This system required the Javanese to grow cash crops, such as sugar cane or indigo, which, although profitable on the world market, were of little practical use to the Javanese. In effect it meant compulsory labor and the exploitation of the entire island as if it were a feudal estate. The system proved profitable for the Dutch, and because it introduced varied crops such as tea and tobacco to local agriculture, it indirectly improved the living standard of some of the people. It also fostered distrust of colonial authority, caused uprisings, and provided the impetus for liberal reform on the part of Dutch politicians in the Netherlands.

Along with the increased demand in the latter half of the nineteenth century for liberal reform came an expansion of direct control over other areas of the archipelago. One of the reasons for this was an unprecedented influx of private citizens from Holland. Expansion of trade required expansion of territory that was under direct control of Batavia to insure stability. Colonial policy improved education, agriculture, public hygiene, and expanded the transportation network. In Java a paternalistic policy was not offensive because its ruling class (the *prijaji*) had governed that way for centuries, but progressive politicians in The Hague demanded that the Indies be administered on a moral basis which favored the interests of the Indonesians rather than those of the Dutch government in Europe. This "ethical policy" became doctrine from about the turn of this century and followed on the heels of a renascence of scientific study of the Indies quite as enthusiastic as the one in the seventeenth century.

The first three decades of the present century were probably the most stable and prosperous in colonial history. This period was also the beginning of an emerging Indonesian national consciousness. Various nationalistic parties were formed, and the Indonesians demanded a far more representative role in the administration of their country. The example of Japan indicated to the Indonesians that European rulers were not invincible. The rapidity with which the Japanese conquered Southeast Asia during the Second World War only accelerated the process of decolonization. In 1945 Indonesia declared its independence, naming Sukarno the republic's first president. The Dutch did not accept this declaration, and between 1945 and 1949 they conducted several unsuccessful military campaigns to re-establish control. In 1950, with a new constitution, Indonesia became a sovereign state.

I offer here only a cursory outline. The historical reality is far more complex and infinitely richer, but this sketch must suffice as a backdrop for the particular type of literature that is presented in this series.

This is a literature written by or about European colonialists in Southeast Asia prior to the Second World War. Though the literary techniques may be Western, the subject matter is unique. This genre is also a self-contained unit that cannot develop further because there are no new voices and because what was voiced no longer exists. Yet it is a literature that can still instruct because it delineates the historical and psychological confrontation of East and West, it depicts the uneasy alliance of these antithetical forces, and it shows by prior example the demise of Western imperialism.

These are political issues, but there is another aspect of this kind of literature that is of equal importance. It is a literature of lost causes, of a past irrevocably gone, of an era that today seems so utterly alien that it is novel once again.

Tempo dulu it was once called—time past. But now, after two world wars and several Asian wars, after the passage of nearly half a century, this phrase presents more than a wistful longing for the prerogatives of imperialism; it gives as well a poignant realization that an epoch is past that will never return. At its worst the documentation of this perception is sentimental indulgence, but at its best it is the poetry of a vanished era, of the fall of an empire, of the passing of an age when issues moral and political were firmer and clearer, and when the drama of the East was still palpable and not yet reduced to a topic for sociologists.

In many ways, this literature of Asian colonialism reminds one of the literature of the American South; of Faulkner, O'Connor, John Crowe Ransom, and Robert Penn Warren. For that too was a "colonial" literature that was quite as much aware of its own demise and yet, not defiantly but wistfully, determined to record its own passing. One finds in both the peculiar hybrid of antithetical cultures, the inevitable defeat of the more recent masters, a faith in more traditional virtues, and that peculiar offbeat detail often called "gothic" or "grotesque." In both literatures loneliness is a central theme. There were very few who knew how to turn their mordant isolation into a dispassionate awareness that all things must pass and fail.

E. M. Beekman

THE ISLANDS

Introduction

ALBERT ALBERTS'S *The Islands* is an outstanding work of Dutch colonial literature. When it was published in 1952, it introduced not only the work of a unique writer but also the only work of colonial fiction that celebrated the Indies as an imaginative island realm. These related stories form a literary archipelago as if in imitation of the island-beads which, strung along the equator, grace the Indian Ocean.

Alberts's fiction resembles a kind of magic: he presents a world which seems designed to imitate reality and then, with an artistic sleight of hand, he transmutes it into something different, something far more impressive than the original material had seemed to warrant. It is, of course, difficult to grasp such vanishing acts, and what follows is by no means intended to give an impression of finality. Auden's definition of "symbol" is relevant when one scrutinizes Alberts's work: a "symbol" is "an object or event which is felt to be more important than the reason can immediately explain . . . and a symbolic correspondence is never one but always multiple."[1] Yet there is a remarkable congruity about Alberts's work which allows one to suggest a possible meaning. It derives from a writer's most indelible influence: his own work. It won't dispel the mystery, but it will give it a shape.

A discussion of Alberts's first published work will be helpful in understanding his other creative prose. Not only will themes and symbols recur in later work, but the style, too, varies remarkably little. From the very beginning the voice was unique and confident and it has remained that way for more than three decades. It comes across as a straightforward discourse written in a plain style that is sober and simple, if not meager. This metonymic style relies a great deal on understatement, even when it deals with the most passionate events. And if it doesn't do that, it will simply state, as if purposely eschewing rhetorical effects.

This is, of course, deceptive. The diction may seem plain, the style artless, but the effect is cunning. Alberts's prose manipulates its inner rhythms expediently, always intent on what it wants to get across. But the style is undeniably sparse, particularly if it is compared with the far more convoluted prose that was current in Dutch fiction at the time of his debut.

As is the case with many colonial authors, it would seem that the impulse came from ordinary, quotidian speech, that simple, vernacular language which the colonists used when they told each other stories. Alberts himself has noted this habit and mentioned Friedericy as a particularly gifted teller of tales.[2] But Alberts has pruned this ordinary delivery of its garrulousness, its gossipy intention and intonation, stripped it to the bone as if deliberately impugning the stereotypical babbling of colonial reminiscences. He has even done the same in his own book of tropical memoirs. His sentences are frequently short, declarative, and in the active voice. This diction is seldom abstruse or aureate, and the meaning of the individual sentences seems clear enough. Dialogue is straightforward and repetitive and is often part of a sentence which describes a simultaneous action. There is a paucity of adjectives and the verb is the syntax's major energizer. The main method for developing longer segments, if not entire texts, is based on contiguity.

Some of these elements of Alberts's style remind one of Hemingway, but I would think, as was true for the American writer, that the prose of the Old Testament—for instance, the clear, sparse delivery of the story of Abraham and Isaac—represents the original source. The tale itself is brief and sober. The syntax is simple, progresses contiguously, and the diction is perfectly ordinary. Yet the dramatic tension is overwhelming. This is accomplished by what is left unstated. Similarly, Alberts's carefully modulated prose seems to have been carved out of silence. His narratives seem to bestow on otherwise simple words an incremental meaning derived from the preceding text. But a great deal remains unspoken, and one gets the feeling that there is a desperate reason for it.

The Islands was not meant to be identified as a description of the Malay Archipelago. Alberts carefully avoided indicators to that effect in order to suggest an indeterminate realm, an insular prototype. That this was deliberate can be deduced from his other collection of stories, *Hurrying in September (Haast hebben in september,* 1975), wherein people, places, and events are carefully labeled. But in one story of the present work ("The Last Island") an island is named. Though most people would not be able to identify it, the island of Raäs does exist. That one clue is augmented by the autobiographical evidence from Alberts's reminiscences about his years in the tropics. Published a decade after *The Islands,* the book was called *Naming Names (Namen noemen,* 1962). When Alberts became suddenly famous in 1975, due to the success of his short novel *The Meeting Room (De vergaderzaal), Naming Names* was republished in 1975 as *Lifted In and Out of Paradise (In en uit het paradijs getild),* a title conferred on it by its publisher.

The adoptive title was apt: Alberts felt like a fairy-tale prince in a magical paradise.[3] Yet the tone of his book of memoirs is casual. Even if his duty assignment as a colonial civil servant was as undemanding as he described in the second chapter, or even if it was a kind of indolent bravura, his nonchalant approach to his office pleasantly mocks the smug pomposity of his colleagues.

The governor of East Java assigned him to a district on the island of Madura. Toward the eastern end of Java, the island's northern coast indents to form a rectangular hook. In that excavated rectangle hovers Madura, over against the large harbor of Surabaya, like a stationary pilot fish nudging its master just above the tailfin. Alberts was assigned to the town of Sumenep, also called Songenep. Madura is some hundred miles long and twenty-four miles wide. The island was already stripped of its trees when Alberts came to live there in 1939. Its poor soil did not allow for much agriculture, and the numerous little rivers washed away whatever small amount of fertile topsoil that was left. It is Madura as the treeless island that forms the background for "The Treasure," one of the tales in *The Islands.*

3

Because it suited his personality, Alberts was fortunate that the jurisdiction of his district included more than forty islands off to the east of Madura.[4] It was these islands, rather than Madura, which inspired the creation of his archetypal realm. After reading *The Islands* one is surprised to know that several of these islands were densely populated. This is true for Sapudi, Goa Goa, and Raäs of the Sapudi archipelago, and of Kangean and Sepeken (which Alberts spells "Sapeken") in the Kangean archipelago. It is clear from his memoirs that two islands, Kangean and Salambu, were his favorites among these fabled islands "which really do not belong in this evil world." Kangean, he felt, was "the most beautiful island in the world," a "paradise," with a bay "far more beautiful than the bay of Naples."[5] The mythical lure of tropical isles is captured in the following brief passage, though it also contains a characteristic note of menace. (A *pasanggrahan* is a rest house for travelers.)

> Ketapang was a little village of no more than ten or twelve houses and the *pasanggrahan* stood on the furthest point of the island, on a hill, a kind of cape. Toward the east one could see the next island only a few miles away; the water between us and that next island was really no more than a narrow strait. A real narrows. During the west monsoon, when it blew hard, the current was so strong that it was clearly visible. Our island had formed a small inlet next to the current, south of the *pasanggrahan,* right at the foot of the hill. The water was perfectly still and there was even a minuscule sandy beach. We sat down on the front verandah of the *pasanggrahan,* stretched our stiff legs, and were suddenly too tired to either take a bath or eat. All we did was sit and look and at a given moment it was dark. Dark and not dark, because we were also treated to the light of the moon. A full one. We looked out over the small, still bay at the foot of the hill in the lee of the sea current. The water glistened a little and the small beach was white. And then a crocodile pushed itself out of the water onto the beach. When it was entirely on the beach it lay still. It didn't move. It didn't even move its head. And we didn't move either.[6]

Except for Raäs, none of these idyllic islands are ever mentioned by name. In his book of memoirs, Alberts states that Raäs was

4

"strange," but his description remains rather vague. It is said to be "low, elongated, without trees, but with many hedges between the yards. The horses weren't so good there, but it didn't matter because Raäs was really small enough to be toured on foot."[7] This is a description also typical of *The Islands:* circumstantial facts which suggest something but which at the same time do not provide sufficient proof to anchor it in reality. Raäs was actually the most agricultural island of the Sapudi group, and had a sizable population.

Alberts deliberately stripped the charted islands of their reality in order to make them more real than that. As Melville wrote of Queequeg's island: "it is not down in any map; true places never are" (*Moby Dick,* chap. 12).[8] As is also true of Maria Dermoût's fiction, Alberts's imaginary archipelago recalls for us why the East Indies were once islands of fable and lore, and why one could call them Holland's Atlantis.[9] Alberts suggested as much in a tale from a later collection—once more emphasizing that his work is of a piece. In "Sea, Unforgettable Sea by Peru" he describes the nostalgic longing of the European when he "stands on his ever western coast, longing for a lost land that lies beyond the setting sun. Perhaps it is precisely this that separates us from Americans. They have two coasts. Standing next to their seas, they can see the sun both rise and set. They know the difference, but it is not an advantage to know everything. God bless Europe and the mystery of nothing but a western horizon."[10] This is one way of explaining why western man searched for the Islands of the Blest, for the Green Island, or why Cook explored the Pacific. This is what Alberts wanted to do with his own "nesomanic" fiction:[11] create a world that, as he described Africa's Cape Blanco, would be "in between a legend and a fog bank."[12]

It is fitting that Alberts's first published work was insular, because it is the basic motif of all his fiction. Mindful of Auden's definition of "symbol," an island can represent a number of things. It can be a utopian retreat from the onslaught of reality, a superior realm of peace and beauty, but it can also be a symbol of isolation, of solitude, of enchantment, and of death. Beyond a geographical enactment of something tangible on an empty sea (as in "Green" or "The Last Island") an island is for Alberts, first and foremost, a state of isolation.

Most of Alberts's fictional characters, including the anonymous narrators of *The Islands,* are what Melville in *Moby Dick* called "isolatoes." "They were nearly all Islanders in the Pequod, *Isolatoes* too, I call such, not acknowledging the common continent of men, but each *Isolato* living on a separate continent of his own" (*Moby Dick*, chap. 27). In the present work we have men who are loners living within their solitude on a geographical equivalent of their emotional isolation. What is ambiguous is that, as soon as they are separated from it, they yearn for it. Alberts, it seems to me, is suggesting that one needs to draw strength from that very fact of separateness. It is just that such strength is rare.

Isolatoes people *The Islands*. In "Green," Peartree is cut off from normal human intercourse except for biweekly visits. He craves human companionship, yet when he is with the narrator he does little to ingratiate himself. He commits suicide when the narrator's selfish insensitivity becomes another act of betrayal—the first was when his wife betrayed him with another man. The narrator himself is defeated by both the tropical forest and his solitude. His derangement becomes poignantly clear when he begins to believe that he can see himself sitting under the lamp—an image of comfort and warmth—even when he isn't there. Naman's house is on an island in "The Swamp." He admits that he can be "nobly alone" there but, of course, he is desperate and mad.

Naman's case is even more painfully illustrative of the life of these isolatoes. Naman is the soul of attentive politeness and is mocked because of it, as if he had the symptoms of some queer disease. Already cut off on the island, he restricts himself even more when he moves away from the people in the village. Human company can be worse than being entirely alone, even though the price may well be madness. "There was no one to talk to in the village and that's why Naman lived on an island in a swamp where there was absolutely no one to talk to, where he saw absolutely nobody. Maybe that wasn't all that crazy. Perhaps it was less bad to be alone than to live in a village where there was no one to talk to." Now he lives with a ghost, a ghost his mind has fashioned for him. And she is a better companion than the Maria of flesh and blood because she doesn't intrude with obstreperous reality. Alberts added even another dimension when he called the self-exiled man Naman. Spelled Naaman in the Old Testament (2 Kings 5:1–27), the name refers to a Syrian leper and means "pleasant" in Hebrew. This is, of course, precisely what Naman was mocked for. In biblical times leprosy automatically meant ostracism, isolation, and an untimely death. The tropical Naman was cast out by human society, too, his solicitousness turned into the reason for his being ostracized, his solitude becoming his quarantine. And for this Naman there is no miracle cure by a prophet. In fact, he has turned his disease into a reason for living, and no longer wants to be cured. Whereas in "Green" the narrator's self-obsession is the cause for Peartree's death, in "The Swamp" the act of kindness of his visit is an intrusion that is not appreciated by his host. Furthermore, the narrator is also infected by Naman's disease and nearly succumbs to it. The presence of Naman's shotgun suggests that Naman might also commit suicide, like Peartree in "Green."

This real, as well as metaphysical, segregation is insinuated in all sorts of ways. In "The House of the Grandfather" the sons of the merchant dynasty have no link of affection with their own fathers but, skipping a generation, love their father's father as if he were their own parent. The downed American fliers in "The Unknown Island" are isolated because they don't know the language of the native islanders. Like latter-day Calibans, they have to acquire a language in order to be set free. The instrument of their release is a telephone and the magic word sounds like the babbling of a child.

Other aspects of the island image can also be found. The funereal island ("Green," "The King is Dead," "The Hunt"), the island of magic ("The Meal," "The Treasure"), or the island as the ambiguous refuge from the occidental world of reality ("The House of the Grandfather"). Good or bad, these islands fascinate because they promise freedom, no matter how ambivalent it might be. Islands will always be a haven for those who feel the desire to escape the mainland. As John Fowles noted in his book on the Scilly Islands: "Islands are also secret places, where the unconscious grows conscious, where possibilities mushroom, where the imagination never rests."[13] This, I believe, is what Alberts tried to convey.

It would require too much space to present all the ramifications of Alberts's work, but one can be sure that certain main motifs are repeated, and that whenever something specific is mentioned it connotes far more than what is immediately understood. Some other suggestions to that effect are made in the notes. One thing is certain, though. As Fowles's description of islands intimates, one cannot remain unchanged after one has been enisled. In the final story of the present work, entitled "Beyond the Horizon," this is made perfectly clear. The people of the mainland—note that Alberts never states that this is Holland—"did not go to the islands. They stayed in this land and have become strangers to us. To us. To all the people on this ship. And we have become strangers to them." This is the general condition for humankind, but this particular passage also refers to the plight of those Dutchmen who had lived in the colonies, were forever changed by them, and came back to a homeland that proved to be a foreign country.

Two images which, together with islands, form a symbolic triad are the sea and ships. But the floating island of the ship, or the isolated life of the seafarer, offers no surcease. In 1979 Alberts published an enigmatic novel about a family of seafarers, with the title *The Dogs Are No Longer Hunting (De honden jagen niet meer)*. The life of the family members who stay on land is described as a lonely one, relieved only by the bittersweet and brief sojourn of the men when they come home after a trip, only to leave again. It is an existence similar to the one in *The Islands* where the link to fellow human beings is formed by the periodic appearance of a ship of the packet line. The novel's Frisian men, women, and children are silent people, not prone to emotional indulgences, closed people who have made a quiet art of enduring. But underneath all that brave silence brews a great deal of tension and pain. The novel, incidentally, ends with one of Alberts's most moving passages, four sentences that are taut with strained composure and with an ineffable love. Captain Wietze arrives home a dying man. He is put in a room near the garden. The wife's youngest son sees his uncle off and when he comes home his mother whispers to him to run and try to bring the uncle back. "And while the little boy walked desperately back and forth by the pier because the ferry hadn't even reached the other side yet, his mother was sitting next to the bed. She folded the blanket back a little and groped for his feet in order to feel if they were still warm. Because she wanted, that he was still alive. Because she loved him."[14] This final homecoming was prophesied by another woman whose husband is also at sea. She tells Captain Wietze's wife that being a mariner is a fine profession except that "every time when they return from there, they have left something behind. Not lost, but left behind. And in the

8

end they are little more than an empty person, one who only asks himself what part of him might still exist beyond that horizon."[15]

This echoes the plight of the isolatoes, of the susceptible colonists who pawned their hearts to *The Islands*. But the sea should, by rights, offer comfort. It represents freedom, it ignores the multiplicity of the civilized shore, "Time notes no wrinkle on [its] azure brow" as Byron stated in *Childe Harold* (canto 4), it has no limitation, and it is formless. But as Auden noted in his essay on the romantics' interpretation of the sea, the very fact that this element is limitless and free makes it also "a lonely place of alienation, and the individual who finds himself there, whether by choice or fate, must from time to time, rightly or wrongly, be visited by desperate longings for home and company."[16] One could say that Captain Wietze should have stayed home and that the narrators of *The Islands* should have remained in Europe. But the response, of course, is that they can't. The distant places have taken too much away from them. They no longer fit—if they ever did. And one should also remember that Alberts described the European as always yearning for "the mystery of nothing but a western horizon." In that same tale in fact, "Sea, Unforgettable Sea by Peru," two men try to escape the "eternal sea, the equable sea, the imperturbable sea" by going inland by bus.[17] But once they're high up in the mountains they get one more glimpse of the sea. They force the driver to stop the bus and they get out. "We looked at the sea. At the enchanting, vast, unforgettable sea of Peru."[18] There is no escape.

In an interview in 1964, Alberts said that the difference between him and the younger generation of writers was that the latter write to liberate themselves (primarily from their youth) while he writes "from nostalgia, that is to say, in order to be imprisoned again."[19] Hence in the story "The House of the Grandfather" in *The Islands*, the eponymous founder of the Taronggi dynasty emerges from the sea to walk to the island with "steps leading him out of the prison that the water had been for him in the final hours, a prison he had gotten used to." And yet, with the first step onto this island refuge, he has begun to yearn, yearn for his country of origin. And over the years the Taronggis become imprisoned by their memory of the ancestral home in Spain, a country and a house none of them has ever seen, except for their castaway forebear. All Alberts's characters do

9

"suffer a sea change" and sometimes even, as Ariel's song rhymes, "into something rich and strange." But they pay the price of exile for it.

There is, however, one figure in Alberts's work who does manage to escape. He does so willingly and in defiance of what society expects of him. It is noteworthy that his solace is in solitude and that the medium of his liberation is a forest. Forests are another major symbol in Alberts's work, and they, too, are linked to islands and to the sea.

The short novel is called *The Trees (De bomen)* and was first published in 1953, one year after *The Islands*. The link between the two works is the color green, especially as a metonym for woods. The story records the emotional bond between a boy, Aart Duclos, and trees over a period of, roughly, twelve years.[20] As usual, Alberts wove all kinds of subtle details in the book, but it is the major elements that concern us here. When he is still small, Aart sometimes anthropomorphizes the trees, which does not seem out of place for a child. But one soon gets the feeling that Aart is perfectly serious about this personal relationship, and that it is not likely to change. What is masterful on Alberts's part is that Aart is a sincere and pleasant child, and that there is never any indication of an aberration, just a pure and simple purpose which will not be waylaid. A teacher, Mr. Barre, gives Aart the nickname "Aardenburg," which in Dutch means a fortress made of earth. The teacher draws on the blackboard a castle with four towers and an earthen wall around it, and Aart proceeds to build this castle in the forest down the road from his house. He does so in an open spot which assumes the characteristics of an island. Within this circle, and within his own castle, Aart is free, himself, and at peace.

This castle is kin to the "Second Java Fort" in the story "The Hunt" in *The Islands*. The descriptions are identical. The two Java Forts were built by a king, but Fort Aardenburg was built by one too. His sister's fiancé, Lamme, tells her that he always had the feeling that Aart was superior, a "grand seigneur" who is not arrogant or conceited, but who has a natural nobility, as if "he is at the head of a retinue of followers."[21] These "followers," it is suggested, are the trees.

Aart's castle and forest in *The Trees* are described for a third time in Alberts's autumnal collection of stories, *Hurrying in September,* in a text entitled "The Autumn of Nostalgia." There it becomes clear that since this particular forest was royal property, it could not be developed, hence it was an arboreal island in the teeming urban sea of modern Holland. Second, Alberts implies that a forest can be potentially recalcitrant. The forests are said to be "capable, and, if necessary, willing to move back into the village and occupy it. This is possible because they feel supported by a mighty army, an unassailable reservoir of tree power." Finally, "a forest in autumn is autumn itself. It is peace, resignation, nostalgia. It is silence and inevitability. There is nothing moribund about a forest in autumn. There may be a dying on the horizon, one that can be seen while walking through a lane at the edge of the forest, and perhaps not even there. But the forest simply enters the night. It creaks and rustles and it lives on. There is nothing mysterious about a forest. Silent houses can be frightening, but a forest never is. It lets us go our own way. But it can make us realize at times the autumn of our nostalgia."[22]

Aart built his fort in the forest in October and returns to it in the fall, some years later, just after he has entered the university. For his teacher Mr. Barre, Aart's forest is hostile because the trees, like nature itself, are indifferent to human existence. One autumn evening he watches the headlights of a car sweeping through the night forest. The light would have startled people but "those damned trees just stand there very calmly. Nothing can upset those damned trees. They do what they want. They're never afraid, never ashamed, never startled." Mr. Barre is, like Aart, a solitary person. There is an understanding and an affinity between the boy and the older man. But Mr. Barre's isolation is, like Mr. Dalem's in *The Meeting Room,* a desperate one, it is not nurtured on individual strength. The implacable forest shows him his fear and desperation. He can never be one with it, never be one with nature, because he can't let it be. When he gives Aart a drawing of the forest, his final act in the book, it shows Aart's open spot surrounded by trees: it is as empty and silent as death.[23]

Mr. Barre is what Aart could become if he allowed society to divorce him from nature. Aart once asked his uncle if he would ever want to be a tree, and got no answer. Aart *can* be a tree, however—metaphorically. After he has registered at the university in the fall, he is subjected to the ritual of hazing. He withstands the humiliations and ridicule with imperturbable grace, and it is clear that he harbors within something that is unassailable, perhaps "an unassailable reservoir of tree power." What the hazing, as a symbol of society, is trying to do, is strip him of his "greenness." Like Joyce, Alberts "passes punplay into ernest" *(Finnegans Wake)* here, because in Dutch this ritual is called *ontgroenen,* literally "degreening." In Aart's case it would not merely degrade him, it would mean surrender to a society that wants to "defoliate the green man" in him, as John Fowles called that aspect in us which should be in unison with nature.[24]

And so, during a night of boozing, Aart gets up and leaves. He hires a taxi to take him back to the forest of his youth. He has the driver stop by the wood. "This is where I live," he tells him. And when he walks through the nightly wood the trees move with and through him. He is at one with them.

In *But the Gold Remains a Gleaming Yellow* (1981), his most recent and most enigmatic novel, Alberts has a phantom king profess: "Fortunate is he who in solitude finds a treasure."[25] (The original sentence has the same ambiguity.) Aart Duclos has found both: sustenance in his solitude as well as an ability to claim a treasure at the heart of it: nature.

In *The Islands,* the European characters have as ready a chance as Aart did. But they won't take it. The narrator of "Green" betrays his dissociation from himself by his contempt for the native population and his proper bureaucratic desire to bring order into his chaotic island world. Through entries in a diary, we are witness to his gradual dissolution. His avenger is the forest, that overpowering green of tropical jungles which Robert Louis Stevenson on Samoa called his "strangling enemy," that was to be combated "with axes and dollars."[26] The Dutch narrator proceeds to do so, hoping to vanquish the forest methodically, building outposts as if to celebrate his conquest. But he experiences a reaction similar to Mr. Barre's: "Here in the Northwood everything stays completely the same and this sameness becomes intensely evident in the green light."[27]

In his obsession to encompass the forest, to own it, as it were, the narrator has cut himself off from his own nature and from that of his fellow man. Fowles noted that trees are "social creatures, and no more natural as isolated specimens than man is a marooned sailor or a hermit." The narrator's obsession to "know" the forest, to get a

purchase on it, to inventory it, blinds him to the need of his fellow in-
mate of the island, a man who is called "Peartree." The narrator has
made the arboreal green an adversary, and the "green man" within a
victim. And the forest takes its revenge. When the narrator thinks he
has bested it because he has advanced through it to reach its furthest
limit, he finds an open space, an emptiness sown with rocks, a petri-
fied landscape as barren as his own nature. It is a landscape of death.

Fowles correctly suggested that the untamed forest corresponds to
the "wildness" of the unconscious, a "mental greenwood."[28] That is
what the narrator is confronted by when he turns to look at the forest
again after he has "conquered" it. He is facing what he has denied in
himself and what he sees is horror, an arboreal version of Conrad's
heart of darkness. "The sky was a moldy gray and beneath that sky,
against that sky, was the forest, a poisonous green in the glaring light
of the gray sky, a layer of slithering, sliding snakes." The face of nature, which was one of kindness to Aart Duclos, has turned here into
a Medusa head that petrifies. Left to himself after his "murder" of
Peartree, his mental greenwood defoliated, desperate for a lightfix to
give comfort in his dead of night, the narrator has nothing left but to
survive. It is a life sentence.

In "The Hunt" the symbolic center of the tale lies once again in a
forest, the same royal wood from *The Trees* and "The Autumn of
Nostalgia." That forest is also the domain of wild boars which were
"part of the forest in the same way as the creaking of trees were part
of it." They are as much a symbol of wild nature as the trees. In this
story the gamekeeper has assumed the role of the categorizing narrator of "Green"; he is the direct opposite of the "natural" animals.
During his first encounter with a boar, the narrator saves the animal
from its pursuers. In the second incident he saves himself, in the role
of the gamekeeper's quarry, within a magic fort in a magic forest.
The final corollary is a fruitless hunt for a boar; at its end the narrator
is mistakenly identified as the quarry and is shot at.[29]

The presence of the boar is a narrative symbol as complex as
Auden indicated. The animal is featured in a variety of myths and
legends. Venus's lover, Adonis, was killed by a boar, and the goddess
commemorated him with the flowers which, red like Adonis's drops
of blood, we call anemones, literally "wind flowers" (Ovid, *Metamorphoses,* Bk. 10). Meleager killed the Calydonian boar although

Atalanta hit it first, but that triumph is also the indirect cause of his death (*Metamorphoses*, Bk. 8). The third labor of Herakles was to capture the Erymanthian boar alive. In northern mythology Frey and his sister Freya rode boars as their mounts, and the animal's flesh was the meat of the gods. Alberts insinuates a number of such aspects into his story. The boar is an autumnal animal. It is traditionally hunted in October, which is also the "season" of Alberts's nostalgic woods. The wild boar was an animal associated with lust and sexuality, for instance in these lines from *Cymbeline* (2, 5, ll. 15–17): he "like a full-acorned boar, a German one, Cried 'O' and mounted." One may note that during the hunt in the Dutch forest, the boar has to be driven from an oak forest close by the house of the girl the narrator was in love with, and one could even suggest that the killing of Florines is, besides other things, the narrator's attempt to revenge himself on Albert, the tenant farmer, because he was preferred by the girl. There is even a link via their names. Albert means "bright" in Anglo-Saxon, while Florines, besides the obvious meaning of "flower," also means "bright" in Latin.[30]

The libidinous aspect is unambiguous in Alberts's story. Florines, who is symbolically identified with the wild boar, is a "pimp" who arranges sex parties in his mountaintop retreat, parties which, even as memories, still resonate with lust. Florines is also associated with the boar by virtue of his name which contains the basic Latin word for "flower," while it is said that in Holland the prolific swine destroy both the gardens of the villagers as well as their "flower beds." It was mentioned that Venus celebrated Adonis's memory with the little red flowers of his blood, and in the *Nibelungenlied* (*Aventiure* 16), when Kriemhild dreams that Siegfried has been killed by a boar, she also sees flowers dyed red from his blood. When the commandant in "The Hunt" flags his battle map, he uses red ones for Florines and white ones for the hunters. Finally, although usually considered a lunar animal, the boar is also associated with the sun, with gold, and with fire. The latter triad is related to sexuality as well. This association would also hold true for the Indies, where the wild boar is found on many islands. For the Malay the *babi utan,* as in some occidental myths, is a superior animal in that he is associated with gold, and gold is both a metal and a color reserved for royalty.[31]

The hunting of Captain Florines is pursued on two levels. At first, the narrator is a most reluctant pursuer because he has been forced into a role similar to the hated gamekeeper. As a government official he is duty-bound to pursue Florines, but it goes against his nature. But he is also excited by the hunt because he, the erstwhile quarry, is now pursuing the hunter. But at the moment of truth, he is the hunter again and feels pity for the hunted animal, a compassion that wells up from the memory of his youth. Yet he kills Florines. The crucial moment comes when Florines turns around, and the narrator looks at something abhorrent, the way the narrator of "Green" turns around to confront the forest and is horror-stricken. It is Florines's face: the face of lechery and salaciousness. This is not unbridled nature or the unadulterated sensuousness of Rima in Hudson's *Green Mansions*. Florines has adulterated it, made it illicit, has merchandised it for profit. It is that face of travesty that the narrator kills with one shot. And one remembers the passage from the beginning, where we are told that Florines shoots wild boars to sell their carcasses to butchers, and that he also hunts women in order to sell them. Florines represents everything that cheapens nature, and in that sense "The Hunt" echoes "Green."

But the narrator himself has also been hunting. He did so in the Veluwe, he assumed the role of the gamekeeper in the Indies, and textual links suggest that he and Florines are, in some ways, alike. And when Florines is burned on the pyre, it is a hero's funeral, it is the roasting of a wild boar, but it also represents the narrator killing himself, if only by proxy.

The chill of the ending is ambiguous, though inevitable and right. As long as Florines's face is averted, the narrator can maintain the fiction that he is paying tribute to his friend the boar with a heroic funeral pyre. Perhaps the burning is also a mourning for his youth, for the innocence of that right royal wood which knew no death and where he could act like Robin Hood and preserve its denizens from harm. For with the firing of the avenging shot he has also killed his better nature. The menacing chill at the end might represent the bitter cold of loneliness. It could, at the same time, refer to Meleager's death: after he has killed the Calydonian boar and his two uncles for the sake of Atalanta, he died from a fire within, the victim of his own mother, who avenged her brothers by relighting the doused wood to consume his life.[32]

If one reads Alberts's work carefully, one begins to discern a circular pattern. The actions of most of his characters seem futile attempts at breaking through something which they won't accept as inevitable. They seem to be wandering through a labyrinth in search of a treasure they believe to be at its center.

In the final analysis this is a flowing back to one's own self. No matter how long it takes or how far they travel they will have to return to where they started. The most obvious representation of this inevitability is the life of a mariner, and it is represented as such in *The Dogs No Longer Hunt:* outward bound means homeward bound. There is a similar structure in *The Islands.* In "Green" a man is carried to the shore of an unknown tropical island and in the end he goes back "Beyond the Horizon," back to the country he came from but which has now become as foreign as that other peregrine shore. This is beautifully set forth in the story appropriately entitled "The Last Island." After roving through the archipelago in search of an island where the best swimmers live, Olon has only sailed home to Raäs via the shortest route. Captain Wietze in *The Dogs No Longer Hunt* tries to find an oceanless existence and hides in Brazil, but he too is brought home because the way forward is the way back. Aart Duclos leaves his forest only to return to it.[33] Mr. Dalem in *The Meeting Room* leaves his mind in order to return to it, although he will never be the same again, as indeed none of Alberts's characters ever are after their peregrinations. They have to learn the truth from "Little Gidding," the last of T. S. Eliot's *Four Quartets:*

> We shall not cease from exploration
> And the end of all our exploring
> Will be to arrive where we started
> And know the place for the first time.[34]

The phantom king from Alberts's last book admonished the councillor that "fortunate is he who in his solitude finds a treasure." The journey through the labyrinth of life should not be embarked upon solely in order to find the treasure at its core, for that treasure might turn out to be fool's gold. The importance of the journey lies in the traveling. This may be what Alberts intended in the story "The Treasure" from *The Islands.* The islands' treasure is not a material one to be dug from its soil, or to be wrested from its inhabitants, but their treasure is the islands themselves or, if one wishes, their nature. The enigmatic ending of the story might suggest that, on a human level, the treasure represents the riches of easing another person's loneliness, if that is possible. The narrator and the doctor appear to be the only ones who understand each other. The others think they have found the elusive hoard in terms of gold (Mr. Zeinal), precious stones (Taronggi III), reforestation (the forester), or minerals (the surveyor). But all these treasures are illusory and count for very little. The doctor and the narrator have nothing, but in the end they share what they have. And sharing food is probably the oldest form of expressing kinship, or establishing a bond. Hence it is fitting that in the last story, "Beyond the Horizon," the doctor is the one man from the islands the narrator remembers with the warmest of feelings. The detail of the splash of rum the doctor encloses in his letter is a poignant one, a gesture saved from sentimentality by the sobriety of Alberts's style. It represents a small cry of loneliness from a paradoxical friendship, indicating a far more painful isolation. By the end of the book, neither the doctor nor the narrator can offer solace to one another anymore.

Profound and complex fiction like this is unlikely to have been "lived" in a biographical sense. It wasn't. Alberts's treasure is his imagination, an imagination that turns the dross of reality into a more lasting gold.

Albert Alberts was born in 1911. He came from a family of seafarers. He felt admiration for the way such marine marriages managed to survive, despite the fact that husband and wife did not see each other for seven months out of the year. "Each one had his own department: the man had his ship and the woman was the captain of the family. Both respected the other's territory."[35] In his youth he lived in Apeldoorn, near the forest that was a royal domain and that became a central metaphor in his fiction.

During the thirties he enrolled as a student at Utrecht University to study "Indology," as Friedericy did. This meant, in practical terms, that he was being prepared for a position in the colonial civil service, a prospect which was well-nigh a guarantee of employment. There was some logic for his choice, since his father was employed as a master by a shipping line that sailed to the Indies, and his two brothers and a sister were already living there.[36] But the Depression intervened and Alberts went to Paris, where he worked in the French Ministry of Colonial Affairs from 1936 to 1939. He wrote about his experience with the Gallic version of bureaucratic ineptitude in a book of reminiscences, written in his inimitable style and enlivened with his irony, entitled *Slipshod (De Franse Slag,* 1963; reprinted in 1975 with a new title supplied by his publisher, *Delivered to France [Aan Frankrijk uitgeleverd]).*[37] During that same time he wrote his doctoral dissertation on two nineteenth-century Dutch politicians who were on opposing sides during a conflict about how to liberalize colonial policies, or, as Alberts put it in his introduction, trying to "kill the colonial goose while at the same time continuing to collect its golden eggs." Published in 1939, it was an unusually compact dissertation, written with panache.[38]

In September of that same fruitful year Alberts shipped out to the Indies. He was stationed in the Sumenep regency on the island of Madura. He enjoyed himself unabashedly, as can be deduced from his description of his first visit to the native regent, Raden Aju, in November of that year, in full uniform, pleased with the pleasant company while listening to a radio playing Dutch popular music in the background: "I looked at my feet. They were encased in black silk socks and black shiny shoes, just the way it should be. And all of this—this sultry dark evening, this palace, this gold, the kris, and the song—all of this was so unreal that I knew I had been turned into a fairy-tale prince. A fairy-tale prince making between two hundred and fifty and four hundred guilders a month."[39] But in March of 1942 the fairy tale turned into a nightmare. Along with his colleagues, Alberts was arrested by the Japanese occupation troops. He was first incarcerated in the Bubutan prison in Surabaya for ten months, then for another ten months in Fort Ngawi in central Java, then for some five months in the infamous Sukamiskin prison near Bandung. After that he was transferred to a concentration camp near Tjimahi, the former garrison town of the Dutch colonial army. In this camp that held more than ten thousand men, he was reunited with his two brothers and met his fellow-writer Friedericy. He barely survived.

After the Japanese surrendered in 1945, Alberts, like the other Dutch prisoners from the Japanese camps, became a helpless pawn during the so-called Bersiap period when the Dutch were trying to re-establish control, British forces were trying to maintain control, and the forces of the new republic of Indonesia were demanding control.[40] He left Indonesia in 1946.

Repatriated to a ravaged Holland, Alberts worked from 1946 to 1953 as executive secretary for an enterprise called the "Kina Bureau."[41] This was a cartel of producers and manufacturers of quinine (*kina* in Dutch), the most effective medicine against malaria. Holland had a virtual monopoly until the fifties, when strong competition from the Belgian Congo weakened its position. The cartel Alberts worked for quietly faded out of existence. His experience of endless business meetings was the basis for his novel *The Meeting Room (De vergaderzaal)*, published in 1974, which describes how a businessman becomes temporarily insane.

Alberts worked from 1953 to 1964 as a journalist and newspaper editor, writing mostly about Indonesian politics. In 1952 he had published the present collection of stories, *The Islands (De eilanden)*, followed in 1953 by the novel *The Trees (De bomen)*. His work was well received—he even won a literary prize in 1953—but it sold very little. During his years as a journalist he also published two books of reminiscences and wrote stories occasionally. Alberts, who must be one of the most unpretentious of writers, wrote these stories for such unobtrusive markets as in-house publications of banks and wine distributors.[42] They were not published in book form until 1975.

After his years as a journalist, Alberts worked for about a decade for the Dutch government in The Hague, in the Ministry of Foreign Affairs. For the last five years before his retirement in 1976 he worked in the translation department, translating official documents from English, French, and German.

When Alberts published his first book in 1952, he was already past forty. *The Islands* was written in a unique style which hardly varied over the next thirty years. For many years he was esteemed but barely known, but when in 1974 he published the short novel *The Meeting Room*, about the brainsick businessman Dalem, he suddenly found himself an overnight success.[43] The year 1975 was Alberts's *annus mirabilis: The Meeting Room* and his two books about his tropical years and his years in Paris were reprinted, while his collection of stories, *Hurrying in September (Haast hebben in september)*, and a historical work entitled *The Dutch Are Coming to Kill Us (De Hollanders komen ons vermoorden)* were published for the first time. In the same year he was awarded the prestigious Constantijn Huygens Prize.

His is a most unlikely Cinderella story (and Alberts a most unlikely literary lion), but his success is a heartening fact nevertheless. Even after 1975 his enigmatic fiction continued to be successful. *The Dogs No Longer Hunt (De honden jagen niet meer)*, published in 1979, was also a best-seller for a while. In the same year he published a nostalgic account of the ocean liners which used to take the Dutch to the tropics: *By Mailboat to the East (Per mailboot naar de Oost)*.

Alberts published three historical volumes which are far longer than his purely fictional works. *The Castricum Hussars (De Huzaren van Castricum,* 1973) is an account of the battle between the combined forces of the French and Dutch republics and an invasion force of British and Russian troops in 1799 near the Dutch port of Den Helder. A most unlikely scenario, though it was one of the bloodiest battles ever fought on Dutch soil. Some twenty thousand men died. The second work of this nature was published in 1975 and dealt with the politically expedient separation of the northern and southern Netherlands between 1585 and 1648; it was entitled *The Dutch Are Coming to Kill Us*. The third, equally long work, about Louis XIV, was published in 1976 under the title *A King Who Did Not Take No for an Answer (Een koning die van geen nee wil horen)*.

Alberts has also published a number of brief historical studies, including a little book about the relationship between Holland and Indonesia between 1945 and 1963.[44] For a man who likes to pretend that he doesn't work very hard, it is altogether an impressive achievement. His most recent work of fiction was published in November 1981 and represents his art at its best. It encompasses all the major motifs which were outlined here—island, sea, labyrinth, gold, bureaucracy, history, vegetation, and parallel time-tracks—in an even more condensed and mysterious tale than is his wont. Its fine, alliterative title—*Maar geel en glanzend blijft het goud*—is lost in translation: *But the Gold Remains a Gleaming Yellow*.[45]

One can tell from this brief biography that Alberts's work is hardly autobiographical as some critics have maintained.[46] To be sure, his fiction has some basis in fact, but that is hardly novel. Except for his seven tropical years, his life has been rather prosaic. Yet he has written a masterpiece of Dutch colonial fiction and is one of the most important writers of modern Dutch literature. Alberts has taken the strands of familiar reality and, like the knot sailors call a crowned knot, twisted and interwoven them into a new configuration that is permanent and can never be unraveled.

But Alberts would demur. With gentle cunning he has always managed to evade critical entrapment. It is perhaps best to conclude with one of his typically evasive answers to a question about literary influence. Alberts responded: "Semarang [a port in Java] doesn't have a harbor. Little boats used to come alongside with things in them. And there was a man, not one of my colleagues but somebody who worked in the salt industry, who wanted to go for a swim very badly. He asked one of the native men who had just gotten into one of those little boats and was about to row away: 'Can you swim here?' And the man said: 'You can.' So he undressed and was just about to jump overboard when he thought: goddamn it, maybe there are sharks or crocodiles. And so he said very quickly, just before he was to jump: 'Are there any crocodiles?' 'Certainly,' said the rower. He had very nicely answered every question."[47]

THE ISLANDS

Green

THE whole morning it has been nothing but coast-
line, an exceptionally pleasant and neat coastline, a real piece of nature with palm trees, but they don't wave.[1] I would like it even more
if they did, and if I did not know that the thick, white line under the
palm trees becomes more and more dirty and dingy as you get closer,
and that filthy huts appear under those same palm trees. I know all
that, and I say goodbye to the captain, which is not necessary at all
because in an hour he will also be going ashore, and I step into a
prahu and we row to the shore.

The sea is filthy already, which does not surprise me, and so shallow that we are already scraping the bottom. The rowers jump out to
push the prahu further, and we are probably still a mile from shore.
At first they wade up to their waist through the water, but the sea becomes more and more shallow and I can already see the legs of the
biggest one, who is walking right next to me. Finally we are perma-
nently stuck.

I see a bunch of people standing under the palm trees, not doing
anything, just standing there, but then I also see that two men are on
their way toward me with a litter. They come alongside the boat. The
litter is a worn desk chair, nailed to two bamboo poles, with no paint
left on it, and with a hole in its cane seat. I sit in it and we wobble
toward the beach and a little later I am standing on the sand that is
just as filthy as I thought it would be.

Opposite me a man who introduces himself: Peartree. He is a col-
league of mine, also living on the coast, but sixty miles further west.
A two days' walk, he says, and I express my admiration at such a
pace. Yes, you've got to be able to walk around here, he says, and

then he asks what I brought with me. And also some beer and gin, I conclude, because I don't know yet what his attitude is toward beer and gin. How much?, he asks. The amount is more than he expected even though I only report half of it, otherwise he'll still be here for another two weeks, and while it is possible, if not probable, that a month from now I will throw myself at any sweaty European as the only white man I have seen for some time, I've had enough for now.

This is the village chief, Peartree says and he points at the front bearer of my chair, and I give him a friendly nod. And now you probably want to know where you're going to stay. He has obviously decided to become more cheerful because he can look forward to beer, gin and a landsman who provided them. I now also notice from his tone and manner that he is nervous, in fact, his nerves are all shot.

We walk on through the palm trees, because my house appears to be beyond the palms in a more ordinary forest. Those palms are like a screen of about a hundred feet between the coast and the forest.

I see my house. It isn't so much a house as a part of the forest, under a lean-to roof, and partitioned into a couple of compartments. There are chairs and a little table in front, and for a moment I imagine that the glasses are already on the table, but it isn't quite as bad as that yet, even though it won't be long now.

The place looks cool and is cool and also quite pleasant. A couple of villagers are watching. They are your servants, says Peartree, your predecessor left them behind. Who was it, I ask. I had met my predecessor some time ago and I know that he's on leave now, but I think it's better to act ignorant like a greenhorn on occasions like this.

Can't remember his name, Peartree says. As a matter of fact, he drank himself to death. I say: that so?, and a little later again: that so? Now he knows that I know that things are tough around here. And perhaps I'm showing that I can handle this, as well as future problems by starting to drink right on top of this. Given the situation, that seems tactless enough. So I say: How about a beer?, and we sit down at the table. Perhaps my predecessor didn't quite drink himself to death, but his servants sure know all by themselves how to find a crate of beer in my luggage, to break it open and to open the bottles. After things have gotten a little friendlier between Peartree and me, I feel that I can leave him alone for a while.

Inside my house I've got to take a breather and I lie down on my bed, that is to say I lie down on the bed in the room where my luggage is. For the first time since my arrival I experience a feeling of loneliness. I lie back on my bed with my hands folded under my head though, naturally, I am ready to jump up at the sound of Peartree's footsteps, because I don't want him to find me here like this. And I think of a girl I once used to know, and I wouldn't mind if she'd walk right in at this moment. I would show her the forest, I do believe that it is quite beautiful really, and we would sit together in the garden, this spot in the green forest. Then the beer begins to take effect, we drank rather fast after all, with the result that I want to keep on drinking.

I go outside and see that I have to restrain myself a little because the captain of my ship has also arrived and he and Peartree are discussing business. Settling old orders and placing new ones. I pour another round and join them to show that I am interested. When I finally realize that Peartree is only talking about private business, I go inside again, but this time I walk out at the rear and into the forest. It really is a very beautiful forest with tall trees that are not too close together, although the crowns touch each other everywhere, with the result that the space beneath them is filled with green transparent light. After I've walked for a while it occurs to me that if I keep on walking I will reach the edge of this forest sooner or later, and that I will sit at the edge of the forest and look out over a wide plain. But right now I don't see my house anymore, so it is better to go back.

Peartree and the captain are at the gin already and the conversation becomes general, stories about other lonely places, stories about big cities, and then the captain says that he has to keep an eye on the time. We take him to the beach and we've had enough to wave him goodbye when he wobbles in his chair to the prahu. I notice with some satisfaction that the village chief is not one of the bearers. Then we go back to the gin.

I ask Peartree about the forest and if there is an end to it. An edge to the forest, I say. He gets up, goes inside, and comes back with a map where he shows me where the edge of the forest is, sixty miles north of the coast. He shows me several places along that edge that are easy to reach as far as the vegetation is concerned. He says: You'll want to get away from that forest every so often.

When it gets dark they bring a petroleum lamp. The thing is hung from an ingenious stand, an iron bar that lies horizontally across another iron bar, which is stuck into the ground. Can't fall over, Peartree says. I ask him if they have also lit a lamp inside the house. He says: yes. I say: because I have to write a letter. To a girl. He says: the boat is already gone and I say: Yes, but. Well, he doesn't give a damn, Peartree says. I bow to him and go inside. It's quite a problem because I'll never find my stationery, oh well, I still have some letters in my pocket and on the back of an envelope I write with difficulty. I'll copy it tomorrow, sweet darling, sweetest darling.

I tell Peartree about the girl, he tells me about his wife, he is divorced, she ran off with somebody else. We might as well not eat and I tell Peartree about the bottle of cognac that should be somewhere in my luggage and is found by my predecessor's servant, damn it, my predecessor must have drunk himself to death after all, the servant hasn't prepared any food either.

A day later.
Today from eight o'clock on is the first day that is completely mine. This day and the following days are my personal property, I can do what I want with them. Now I can cut through the narrow strip of palm trees to the sea and then walk for some distance along the beach to where there are no huts anymore, lie down on the sand in such a way that the shade of the palm trees covers me. Because I've got a head you won't believe. Peartree has left. He was up at six, and so was I for that matter. He was drinking coffee in the garden and looked very angry when I wished him good morning. Angry and also very haughty, he was put out, of course, about having confided in me yesterday. We drank our coffee together and I wasn't in such great form myself, rather stiff really, because last night I had also revealed my intimate problems to him without holding back, and had sworn that I would follow his advice.

We remained sitting there silently and ill at ease and if Peartree had only said something like: Come on, cut it out, we would have grinned despite our sore heads and would have rubbed our sandpaper tongues against the roofs of our mouths and kept silent and everything would have been all right, except for the emptiness I would have felt after his departure.

But Peartree snapped at me. He called for the village chief, gave instructions, and left at eight o'clock. His attitude spared me the sadness of a farewell. I am beginning to feel better already and think that it's quite nice around here. Even the palms are waving.

The sea is very wide and far, not a ship in sight, that's probably always the case around here. There are a few prahus on the beach, those things you've got to push, with an outrigger, they won't get very far in them and I wonder how the fishing is, to hell with it, I don't feel like getting involved now already with the problems of the village's economy. I'd rather look at the sea, just like that, as if it's the sea and close my eyes and go to sleep.

I wake up with the sun on my legs and then the feeling of owning this as well as the following days has become burdensome enough that I go look for the village chief. He tells me all about the prahus and the amount of fish they catch. About what they eat and what the forest produces. How purchasing and transportation are arranged. He tells me all sorts of other things but there's soon an end to what I can take in. So I ask him about the extent of the forest and I point in a northerly direction. I know from Peartree that the edge of the forest is another sixty miles, but I secretly hope that somewhere there will be an open space before that. Because this is one of the few resolutions from yesterday I want to act on: to build a little house near an open space in the forest or better yet at the edge of the forest with a view of the free plain. The village chief looks doubtful. He doesn't know about that, he says. Can't we search for it?, I ask. He looks even more doubtful and says again that he doesn't know about that. But I'll get it out of him. I ask him if there are any people living farther up north who might know. Oh, he says, I don't know and this time it sounds so pitiful that I stop trying. It might cost me my popularity.

I walk with him to his village, brown huts, filthy children, and I keep on walking and I make sure that I stay a couple of steps in front of him, otherwise he will take me to his house, his filthy house, to drink filthy coffee out of filthy cups and to sit in a rickety chair on a stinking front porch. But then he suddenly darts in front of me and he points his thumb so politely and obsequiously at a house, his house, that I smile amiably and, thanking him kindly, go inside. He orders coffee, takes the cup from the hands of a boy, probably his son, and puts it down in front of me. He should also sit down, I say. Oh well, blood is thicker than water, for him as well as for me, but the day is no longer my property, I'm well aware of that.

We've become polite neighbors now. I ask the same questions as before, but this time in the affirmative. I say: The fishermen never go very far away from the coast? He agrees and nods his head like a village schoolmaster who, years later, has an old student come back to visit him from the big strange world out there. Yes, I say, and the resin from the forest is brought here. By whom? I suddenly ask straightforwardly. By our people, he says somewhat surprised. So they do go into the forest? Yes, he says and he points west. And there?, I ask, and I point north, but no, he is not sure about that, he says evasively. And the resin is picked up here by the ship, I say conciliatingly again. Yes, he says. Every six months? Every six months, he repeats with satisfaction. Is that your son? Yes, it is his son, and he's given my empty cup and returns it filled.

In the afternoon, after a meal, I sit down behind my desk, the desk of my predecessor. I take four empty notebooks and write on the first one: *Fishery Report.* I'll pay close attention to that, the number of fishermen, what percentage they are of the total population. And the amount of fish they bring in, of course. And the kind of fish, in short, a thorough report. On the second notebook I write: *Forest Products.* About the expeditions they make, the amount of time they stay in the forest, about what they have stored and the different types, about the prices given by the dealers.

The third notebook becomes: *In General,* and the fourth, I thought that up this morning, is going to be something completely new: *Timber Crop.* As far as I know, they don't fell trees here, even though it is perfectly suited for it, anybody can see that. There must be a special reason for it, transportation problems or something like that. Maybe the wood is not suitable at all, too light or too heavy or whatever. Now that I think about it more, it does not seem such a great idea after all.

Then I realize something. The village chief is always talking about the western forest and I want to go to the northern forest, he doesn't. But what's in the east? I get up and walk outside. Amazing how cool it stays here in this green tempered light. I follow the demarcation between the forest and the palm trees, with the sea constantly in sight, and I walk this way for half an hour, then everything ends and there's only the sea. The sea, which makes a sharp turn north. Hence there is no eastern forest, which is one complication less and one added obligation, because I have no choice now, I must explore the northern forest. It is always that way in life, fewer complications, more obligations.

When I am sitting in front of my house in the evening, with the lamp hanging from the stand, I think of Peartree for the first time since he left. Peartree is about halfway now. He sleeps in the forest, in the western, not the northern forest, and I turn my chair about forty-five degrees so that I face in that direction, north. After I've sat like that for a while, I feel restless and uneasy and I realize that I'm sitting with my back turned to the door, the door of my world. My world is the forest and the door is the beach, the spot where I came ashore yesterday and where other people too, strangers, can land and force themselves into my existence. I turn my chair back to its former position in order to keep an eye on the door. Everything has its proper place now. The west, that is Peartree, that's where he really belongs. The north, the unknown, what I am looking forward to, that belongs. The east, that is Nothingness, that also belongs. And the south, that is the door, and what lies beyond it must remain locked out. I sit in the night and look and see Peartree, thirty miles farther, if he hasn't lied. Annoying Peartree, but you also belong.

A day later.
This morning I invite the village chief to discuss the particulars of my first trip to the forest. While talking, I point west and not north, and he is very happy about that. I hear that we will be visiting some second-rate villages, temporary settlements of the people who gather forest products. We will only be away for two days, staying over only one night, because this is the first time. I don't want to do everything at once and I try to make it clear that Peartree's pace is too fast for me. The village chief, who is my guest now, is completely in agreement with me.

I wonder if we can leave this same afternoon, but I restrain myself just in time, because that would be incredibly dumb and contradictory, to hurry like that. The truth is that the chief's painstaking and endless planning for the trip bores me, because I am not looking forward to the afternoon and evening.

Completely uncalled for: in the afternoon I lie down on a long chair beneath the green with a new detective novel, and for three full hours I read attentively to the end. To the end of a day filled with beauty, to the beauty of the evening, of the silence of the lamp and its light.
Of the silence.
Of the yellow light.

A day later.
This is the day of my first journey. More than ever before I feel the slight but invigorating agitation always associated with travel, because this is travel at its purest, its noblest form, indeed, the form of my journey is noble, ancient and full of tradition.

Up front goes the guide, the scout, walking thirty feet in front of me. In its archaic form this distance would have been a day's travel. My journey is somewhat stylized. This includes where the village chief should be. While he should really be walking a few steps in front of me, he has joined the scout, what one could call the informal style.

I come after him, surrounded by the wall and moat of distinction, I, the prince from the distant court, centuries ago. Respectfully behind me come some lesser dignitaries, members of the village council, if I am not mistaken. There might be some private, well-to-do resin gatherers among them. They have a right, of course, to be part of my retinue. And finally, the train of this retinue is made up of a number of bearers.

We have followed the coast for some time but now, to my great satisfaction, we have changed direction and are heading inland. The forest, as well as the ground cover, becomes denser here, it becomes darker, more ordinary, a less transparent green. In this way we come rather suddenly to our first village. Friendly scouts approach us and there's a great deal of interest when we enter the settlement. I am happy to sit down, but otherwise it's not much around here. The Northwood should be better and more beautiful.

We eat, we rest, do some business, and in the afternoon we go on.

Excellent village chief. He has picked a good place to stay overnight. The second village when we arrive in the late afternoon is large and clean, and the gentleman who receives us is almost dignified. An oily, polite, fat, and doubtlessly rich gentleman is the chief of this second settlement. He looks as if he knows everything that is worthwhile to know in these parts, and when I invite him and some other gentlemen to have a smoke with me after dinner, I feel that I have to take advantage of this opportunity. Forgive me, village chief of mine, but I cannot pass up this opportunity.

This is a fine and large settlement, I say, almost as fine as the big village. They grin and scratch themselves. I point northwest and ask if there are any more settlements there. Yes, two more. And in the northeast?, I ask and I point in that direction and look only at my fat host. He grins and says, he isn't so sure.

There's only one settlement there, my own village chief says. Sometimes people live there and sometimes they don't. We don't know anything else about it.

There is something unmistakably sad and disappointed in his tone of voice when he says this, and his manner is really very dignified. That's why I bow politely in his direction and change the subject to something more neutral: the history of his people.

A day later.

I am back home and it is evening already and the lamp is already brought outside. It seems there is still some cognac left and I finish it. It's quite a lot of cognac. I sit down with my back to the south, because I have to chase away my fear, I've got to steel myself against fear. Because I have to become a courageous man.

There are two possible courses open to me. First of all, I could go to Peartree and ask him the necessary information about the Northwood. He would do that for me. He will probably tell me that one or more nomadic tribes are to be found out there. If I want to have a closer look at these nomadic tribes, Peartree will either approve of it or think it's ridiculous, probably the latter. The other possibility is not to mention anything to Peartree, and that's what I'll do. Because I don't see how I can make it clear to Peartree that I'm not going there for those nomadic tribes, that I couldn't care less about them, that things would be a lot quieter if they weren't there. I can't make it clear to Peartree that I want to reach the edge of the forest, that I want to walk ten, twenty, a hundred yards into the open plain. Then I will turn around to this green forest. No, I will not turn around, not at first, when I come out into the open onto the plain. Perhaps there'll be a hill, I'll climb it and cheer, I'll shout, as I would never dare do inside the green.

Or I'll be silent and take a deep breath, as I would never be able to do in the green light. And when I have drunk my fill of light and distance, I will turn around, raise my glass and laugh and call out: I see you, green forest.

I am having a lot of trees cut, a lot of wood, and I am having a house built, so large and wide that it spreads low against the sky. The entrance on the forest side and a wide terrace on the north side. And a basement, that's a good joke, damn it, I always build houses when I am drunk, damn it all.

A day later.
Today I carefully examine the business affairs of the village, the supply of resin in storage for shipping, the food situation, the general state of health. The village chief accompanies me everywhere. The Northwood is not mentioned anymore, the man deserves it. I try to give the impression of being strictly businesslike, the village chief must be able to count on me, he must be able to trust me.

At home I fix up a little office, pull out my notebooks, and begin my reports. I calculate, I estimate, I make plans. I hesitate for a moment when I hold the notebook *Timber Crops* in my hands. I put it away again. I really don't know anything about wood, and I never will. I don't know the name of even one tree in this area. I'll discuss this matter with Peartree some time.

In the late afternoon I am overwhelmed by an uncontrollable desire to walk into the forest. It is four o'clock and I decide to walk north for an hour. That way I'll still be able to get back before dark. This walk is a serious matter.

It is remarkable how little the forest changes in this direction. It does not become dense and the ground cover stays the same, the light stays the same, everything stays the same, and I am no exception. When I am in my house, in the village, or during the journeys with the village chief, scouts, and the rest, I change like a chameleon. I am courteous, bored, resigned, interested, miserable, drunk, all depending on the place and circumstances. Here, in the Northwood, the place and circumstances stay completely the same and this sameness becomes intensely evident in the green light.

I wonder how I will mark where I'm going in order to be able to find it back again later, but it's impossible. After an hour I turn back, nothing will come of it in this manner. But after another hour I'm still not home. A compass would be useful here, but I do not have a compass and I am lost. When it is completely dark, I can only grope my way and I am very scared until I see a light shining relatively close by. I stumble in its direction, it is the light from my own house, of course, what else could it be.

Sitting under the lamp after dinner, I consider the possibilities. There aren't many. This afternoon I went about three miles north, that is three out of the sixty that lie between my house and the edge of the forest. If I walk six hours a day, it'll take me a week coming and going, and even then I will have to really work at it. I can't do this alone, I really can't do this alone.

A week later.
I'm going to see Peartree today and I really want to. I make an arrangement with the village chief that we'll take at least three, or if we like, four days walking to get there. If it's the latter, he says, we have to stay at least once outside a settlement, that is to say, spend the night in the forest. I ask him if he has anything against it. He says: No, I don't but perhaps you do. I can never figure out if these people are serious about something like this or if they hate not sleeping in a settlement. So I say: I don't mind doing it in three days. He says: If you want to do it in three days, we can do it in three days, and sleep in the settlements. But I say: If you'd rather take four days, it's really no problem for me to sleep in the forest. That's that, I've put the burden of sincerity on his shoulders. Hurrying like that doesn't prove anything, I say. No, he says, it doesn't.

Finally I have confided in him and told him that I would actually enjoy spending a night outside a settlement. He has nodded and smiled in a friendly manner. He is really an amiable character.

My retinue is a little bigger than the last time, there are more people carrying provisions. I join the vanguard. Today we are walking to the first settlement, the same one from the last journey. Then we continued in the afternoon, now we are resting. I see that I've made a good decision when I divided the whole journey into four stages. The village chief and the other gentlemen don't like to exert themselves needlessly either, and when we are sitting together in the evening, they are more talkative than last time.

A day later.
We continue in a westerly direction. I think we are following the beach at a relatively short distance. I ask the guide. He says: Yes, the beach is very close. The forest does not resemble my Northwood in anything. It is much denser, including the ground cover. We walk along a worn path, worn by my predecessors, worn by Peartree, worn by his predecessors, on assiduous journeys with gin at the end.

The settlement we arrive at toward the end of the afternoon betrays Peartree's presence. There is a guest house with all kinds of handyman's touches, such as chairs with ashtrays on the armrests, or kobolds by the washbasin holding a stick between them to hang a towel from. A lamp in a corner is again a kobold on a table holding a lantern high. But why should this be Peartree's work? It could just as well be the work of a teetotaling predecessor, which is really far more likely. A calm, levelheaded person, who puts ashtrays on armrests and who doesn't smoke. He puts a lamp together as if for a joint but he doesn't drink. It is a pretty gloomy place.

I have to meet a settlement chief here I have never met before. This is the third one, a replica of the fat oily host of my overnight stay on the first journey. So here you can still find resthouses with your typical innkeeper.

We have to have a smoke again, although I'm not quite up to it, I'm not up for anything and I go to bed early.

A day later.
Today, at the end of the day's march, we will spend the night in the forest. I get up early and drink coffee. The village chief comes to ask if I might want to leave already. I say: Fine, and we're on our way. The forest is the same as yesterday but in the afternoon we are walking among palm trees. I ask how that is possible. The palm forest is much

wider here than by us, the village chief says. But we are close to the sea, I say. Yes, we are very close to the sea. And how far from the big village? Yes, we aren't that far from the big village any more.

I keep up appearances and nod carelessly, and then we walk another two hours under those damned palms and then we are at Peartree's. I am dead tired and Peartree is loud and jovial.

Go on, he says, freshen up a bit. I was right when I thought that you'd need three days.

I enter his house. I notice that I am putty in the hands of the village chief; that's the way it'll have to be. Peartree's house is bigger and painted darker than mine, brown, rather somber, but it is divided the same way. It is near a kind of square and the whole place makes a martial impression. Peartree had a square section of forest chopped down, and the soil was turned over, but it's full of weeds now. Among those weeds, right in front of the house, are two chairs and a table with glasses and bottles. A beer, Peartree says. Ha-ha, a beer. He's ahead of me. I sit down, stretch my legs, and take a deep breath. The sun shines low over the trees at the edge of the square. I say: You've got it pretty good here and I wave at the open space before me.

What?, he asks. The forest?, and he begins to laugh out loud. I say: No, what I really mean is, that you cut down quite a piece of it. Oh, it was already there when he came here, he says.

You've been here half a year now, right? Half a year, he says, half a year and then another half a year and then we go. Go.

If the tour of duty is a year then, I ask. Peartree scrutinizes me. A year?, he mutters to himself. Yes, of course, a year. Just imagine, for chrissake, if it was more than a year.

I tell Peartree about my experiences with the village chief. Of course, he says, they can't stand long marches, but they'll always manage to get out of sleeping in the forest.

Who put up the guest house where I slept last night?, I ask. Don't know, Peartree says. Was there already. For that matter, I also had one put up in the northwest corner of my section.

How do you do that, I ask. What?, Peartree asks. Have a house built like that? You give orders, Peartree says. So I give orders. Ah, life isn't all that complicated. The lamp is brought outside. So they bring the lamp outside here too, but damn it, I'd really like something to eat. I'm starving. Peartree thinks eating is ridiculous, but all right, all right, he will have them get something.

But how can it be so quiet here? Yes, quiet, when the lamp swings back and forth, there are no tree shadows to swing along with it. The lamp swings in a void.

The ship will be back in two weeks, Peartree says, and then five more ships, and I'm on my way. But it's really not so bad around here, right? Visiting each other every two weeks, imagine, every two weeks you have people visit you in your little parlor, it makes you want to swear a blue streak.

A man could damn well take it, if Peartree kept his trap shut. There are even some stars in the sky. Stars flicker and shine. Peartree shuts up. It's not so bad at all if Peartree talks. Let him talk. I ask him: Peartree, that wood you cut here? I didn't, Peartree says. I say, that wood, in short, and I wave with my hands, could it be used for lumber? He doesn't know, he says. I want to cut some, I say. Chop the whole goddamn forest down, Peartree yells, beat the hell out of that entire forest! Can it be used for carpentry?, I ask. I don't know, Peartree says.

A day later.
But it is still beautiful this morning, that empty piece of land before me, bordered by straight tall trees. Behind me I hear Peartree stumbling around in the house. He comes outside, grumbles when I say good morning, and flops down in a chair. At first he doesn't say anything, we are both quiet, because I don't feel so great myself. It is amazing to see the sun come up and not as at my place, where green light keeps on becoming a brighter green.

Have you been on tour already?, Peartree asks. I fill him in on the adventures of my two-day journey to the northwest. That's all?, he snarls. There are two other settlements, I say, half helpfully, half guiltily. Peartree sniffs contemptuously. And the other way?, he asks. There's another one of those half-deserted places. Didn't you go to take a look? The village chief doesn't seem to feel like it very much, I say as carelessly as possible, but it sounds rather weak. And I feel weak, also confused. My secret plan to make the Northwood a fairy-tale sanctuary for myself is being roughly exposed. Are you such a jerk that you let some village chief boss you around?, Peartree asks.

I say: no. I still wouldn't mind going there. I'd do that. Peartree says. You're gonna get into trouble.

He probably sees me slowly get red, because his last words sound a little friendlier. He's probably thinking: Maybe I was too tough. And now he's afraid that I will get angry. Or he's simply good-natured. But I am thinking something entirely different. I think: Damn it, always the same thing. Because this is not the first time that I clearly miss a chance to realize one of my fantasies.

But it is a passing annoyance. When I reach the big settlement in the evening with the handyman's guest house, I have already fitted the incident into the picture I have of my Northwood. It is and remains a fairy castle with its entrances completely overgrown.[2] Peartree's big mouth has cut a hole in this barrier. Onward.

Two days later.
The rest of my trip back I did in two days and when I come home in the afternoon, I am completely used to the green again and I sit contentedly in my chair in front of the house, when the lamp is brought outside and the play of the tree shadows begins. For the moment I've had enough of ranging in forests. In ten days the boat will arrive. In ten days Peartree will come here. He will ask: Have you been north already? I will say: Yes, I have searched for a suitable spot for a settlement. This is excellent. An excellent plan.

Twelve days later.
The ship has come and gone. I witnessed a replay of my own arrival. Everything was so much like the first time that it frightened me, frightened and depressed me.

Peartree was here for two evenings. In two weeks I will go to Peartree. In a month the ship will come again; third performance.

In the evening I leave my house at the back. The forest is black and impassable. I wander through the trees along the side of my house to the front. I stand behind a tree and look around the trunk. In front of the house in the forest the lamp is shining, in its circle of light is a table and a chair, an empty chair. It won't be long now before I will see myself sitting in the chair while I stand behind a tree and carefully look around the trunk. I wish that there wasn't a lamp burning but a

...old was dancing around it, singing: No-
...ows, that my name is Rumpelstiltskin.[3] It
...more natural.

damn soon,

...chief come to me. I have been ordered, I tell him, to
...dements, and I point in the fatal direction. He is fright-
en... ...nges for a moment. He gives me a long, sad look. I say:
Well, n... ...ing we can do about it, and then I shake my head a bit. I
wish I had never mentioned the Northwood to this man. Until his dying day he's going to regard this assignment as some kind of trick.

The question arises whether there is something I should do myself,
but I wouldn't know what it possibly could be. You give orders,
Peartree says. Are they going there now and are they taking building
materials with them or do they get that on the spot? I would imagine
the latter.

A week later.
In the final analysis it all went rather smoothly. I wanted to have the
first settlement built about twenty-five miles due north. That would
also be just fine, said the village chief, but there was already a settlement around there. When did that happen?, I asked. Yesterday or the
day before yesterday, maybe I would like to have a look one of these
days.

And now I sit under the lamp, and what am I doing? I am singing softly to myself out of satisfaction and relief. The village chief is
a real good person. He still regards the orders I received and which he
passed on as a trick invented by me, but he considers it an admirable
idea on my part to do it in this manner, that I didn't bark the order at
him to begin the expansion at my very first appearance. He hopes
and trusts that we can haggle about the number of new settlements.
Surely there won't be more than two, he thinks. And for one of these
he has earmarked the abandoned settlement that is supposed to belong to a nomadic tribe. This nomadic tribe is nonsense, of course, it
was those gentlemen all along, until they got sick of it. It was their
fear of the unknown forest. The village chief and I, we both have followed the path of least resistance, la de da. But it is much better this
way.

Two days later.
This morning I'm going to see the village chief to arrange for my first journey to the new settlement. We are now so polite to each other, the village chief and I, that I think it better to warn him a few days in advance. Then he can prepare things out there at his leisure, because it isn't even half finished, of course. Once again I regard my impending journey as a pleasant adventure. I really should go to Peartree, but I am putting it off for a week.

Two days later.
We are on our way. The settlement is some thirty miles away, an impossible distance to cover in one day, but thirty miles means half the distance to the edge of the forest. When we arrive this evening, I will reward the village chief by reducing the number of new settlements to be built from three to two.

I am on my way in my magic forest, I walk between the trunks and look around me. There still is no ground cover and now I know why. The ground is rocky. In any case, a lot of large stones are partly buried in the soil and partly visible above it, it is a marvelous forest. Straight trunks, green light, always the same, and it must be very ancient. It is Time itself, I say laughing. Ancient, green, and always the same.

We finally reach the settlement, a couple of somber huts in the darkening forest. I am too tired to eat and I only recover a little in the evening, when I sit on the small porch and stare in front of me into the dark. It is always the same.

A day later.
I sleep late, afterwards I take care of the more urgent matters, jot down data, give my approval for the appointment of a settlement chief. Not until the afternoon does the realization of where I am really strike me. This is the Northwood. If I get up early tomorrow morning and head north all day, I can reach the edge of the forest. For a moment I am tempted to call my village chief and give him the order for the journey. It won't work, there are too many problems. And I also have to go to Peartree. Damned annoying, those visits, but I can't back out of them, ridiculous, forsaken by God and man alike, and I have to hurry to pay a visit.

Two days later.

My legs still bother me from that walk of twice thirty miles. I have been loafing and fooling around all day, with nothing to do really. I won't go to Peartree tomorrow.

Twelve days later.

I ended up not going to Peartree at all and tonight, two days before boatday, he comes walking through the forest. I didn't see you, he says. The work in the forest has kept me, I say. It satisfies him. He is simply nervously pleasant.

Four days later.

Today I walked four hours out and back in the Northwood. It is a marvelous forest in all its similar infinity. If I walk here, or if I walk thirty miles farther down, it's all the same, nor can I change myself during that time.

Three weeks later.

I am in the Northwood, three miles from the border. The second settlement has been built and I will be at the border in one hour. I walked away quietly this morning. I want to be alone when I reach the edge of the forest, when I cross the border. The forest finally changes. It seems as if it enshrouds itself before it will disclose its secret. There are a lot more bushes and it becomes hilly.

In a while I will see the dawn, the dawning of light. And it is already growing lighter.

I will have a house built out there. It will not have a front or back, no preference for forest or open plain. I will know how to be generous after my conquest of the green forest. If need be, I will have the house built round, that is an idea, a round house with a round porch around it.

And then it is light, then I can see the open plain. I begin to run, I trip, I almost fall, but then it is light. It is exactly the way I pictured it, it is truth, I sing, I shout, I am saved.

I stand still, panting, under an enormously wide sky. This is it, then, so this is it.

A great bare land, with many stones, big stones, hilly, with hazy blue mountains in the distance. I walk on now, but more slowly. I also notice that there is no sun. The light is sharp, I don't notice it otherwise, in the forest. I walk on, I know that I have to go back, that I can't stay yet, forever, but just for a moment, just a moment longer, like a child before going to sleep. I sit down on a stone. Where have I seen this before, I am thinking.

Stonehenge, maybe, where Merlin stayed, in a picture in a geography book.[4] There are really huge stones here. And those mountains form an orderly and neat demarcation. I have no desire at all to start also constructing a fantasy about what could possibly lie beyond them. Let's leave well enough alone. Now I know what lies beyond the forest and that will have to be enough. I am behind the forest. And then I turn around to the forest.

Three days later.
I just got home. The village chief and the bearers went home. I cannot ask anyone to stay with me. It wouldn't help anyway. I cannot ask anyone to stay, I can't tell anyone what I saw, when I stood outside it and turned around to the forest.

The wind was blowing when I stood there outside. I had not noticed it as long as I was in the forest, but it was blowing.

The sky was a moldy gray and beneath that sky, against that sky, was the forest, poisonous green in the glaring light of the gray sky, a layer of slithering sliding snakes.

I stood outside it and I was terrified. I wanted to run away to the blue mountains, but it wasn't possible, oh God, of course it wasn't. I had to return, had to walk toward this awful creature with open eyes and enter it, and never, never shall I know again the peace of the green tempered light, now that I know what is above me.

A day later.
This evening I sit on my bed with my head in my hands and a little later I walk out of the house at the back and go between the trunks to the front. I am not afraid in the evening or at night, because the green snakes above me are then as dead. I stand behind a tree and look at the circle of light of the lamp. A table and a chair. Then I go back again along the same path. It is a game that I play again every evening. I am going crazy, I think. Tomorrow comes the ship.

A month later.
I walked all day yesterday and today and this evening I'll be back in my village.

The ship has also been, yesterday. I did not think of it, but the ship has also been here.

It is already dark by the time I arrive home. The lamp is not shining and it is very quiet. I sort of counted on Peartree still being there, but there is no one around. It is actually pitch black. Yes, it is pitch black. I take out my flashlight, find the lamp, light it, and take it outside. When I want to hang the lamp from the stand, I see that I can't, because Peartree is hanging from it.

> And now let sweet and low.
> And now let sweet and low
> and now let sweet and low
>
> Vineflower, swingflower
> Vine in the swing in the vine in the swing in the vine in the swing.
> Vineflower.
> In the flower.
>
> And now let sweet and low[5]

How dark it is, they all took off, and I have left my lantern behind, back there, I have left it hanging. Oh God, I have left Peartree hanging, for how long, at least half the night, I murdered him. If only he hadn't been dead when I arrived. It was his intention, wasn't it, rien que pour vous servir, mon très cher. À la lanterne, Peartree. I am laughing my head off. If, ha-ha, your name is Peartree, then you're going to hang yourself from a tree, ha-ha. Oh well.

But shouldn't he be taken down now? Damn it, I can't find the lamp, I really can't. Otherwise I would have gone to the village chief a long time ago. I can't leave. Wouldn't mind getting out of here. Stop bugging me. I'm afraid, I don't give a shit. I'm afraid. I don't want light. I don't want to see Peartree hanging there. I don't want light.

Hours later.
Oh God, I've been drinking like a lunatic. It is completely light now, perhaps it's afternoon already. Peartree is gone. He's not hanging

there any more. They put him down in an empty house. I write a statement and have a couple of witnesses sign it. I let them put down a cross, which isn't right at all, but it will have to do.

I have to have a grave dug, but that's been done already, the village chief says. I ask about a coffin. They bring one. Jesus, that will never do. We'd have to put him straight up, we'd have to put him straight up and give him a good whack on the head so that his knees will give, maybe it will work then. It will never work.

I say: Another coffin and I give the measurements, seven feet long, two feet wide and deep.[6]

They really did make another coffin. Now Peartree has to go in, but I don't see how, I am a creep, a shitface, I don't see how, but he has to, the poor bastard, poor bastard.

We go to the house, the coffin is carried behind me. I've brought a cloth to put over the coffin.

In the house two tables are pushed together, they've put Peartree on top of them, wrapped in a sheet, but his head sticks out. I quickly put a handkerchief over it, it's even respectful.

I ask for a minute of silence and after that we pick him up, with me at his feet, and we put him in the coffin and the coffin is nailed shut.

We carry him to the grave, of course it is much too small, it was measured for the other coffin. They dig. Clumps of earth fly out of the hole and finally it is done.

Two ropes around the coffin and then we let it down. I am standing near an open grave. Our Father, I say, who art in heaven. When I turn around, I notice that my legs are still drunk.

I leave the lit lamp hanging from the standard like before. Because I am still alive.

The King Is Dead

WHEN I came to the island in November, the King was eighty-two years old. I didn't know that. I didn't even know the King existed. I was much too busy getting used to the fact that I had an office, a high, whitewashed room with maps on the walls. Maps of our island and of the other islands around it. And that my clerk sat behind me in an identical room, my friendly clerk who actually knew everything much better than I did, but never let it show. He knew the King, of course. I didn't at first. Not even after having stood eye to eye with him. That was on the first of December. On that day I was told, at around ten o'clock, that Mr. Solomon wanted to speak to me and I said: Ask Mr. Solomon in. I was sitting behind my desk, ready to stand up and walk toward the visitor. I said: Hello Mr. Solomon, and I walked over to him and I shook his hand and I helped him to a chair.

Because Mr. Solomon was old. Old, yellow, and extinguished. He was wearing a yellow suit and a yellow shirt without a tie and a round, yellow hat which he took off after he had saluted me.[1]

Mr. Solomon is a retired sergeant-major bandmaster, my clerk said.

Mr. Solomon laughed, first at my clerk and then at me. His head was bald and so old that the wrinkles were already beginning to sag away.

Mr. Solomon comes by every month to pick up his pension, my clerk said.

Mr. Solomon laughed again.

As long as he isn't sick, my clerk said. Mr. Solomon is very sick sometimes. How is your health, Mr. Solomon?

Mr. Solomon laughed as though someone were telling a joke, but he did not say anything and my clerk didn't press him for an answer.

I understood that it was my turn now. I said: You are pretty close to sixty, aren't you, Mr. Solomon?

Mr. Solomon laughed again, but this time first at me. And my clerk said: Mr. Solomon is eighty-two. Mr. Solomon nodded proudly a couple of times and I clapped my hands in astonishment. Meanwhile my clerk had fetched the ledger. He wrote something in it and then gave his pen to Mr. Solomon.

You must sign here, Mr. Solomon, he said.

Mr. Solomon put his hat on the floor and carefully leaned over the book. My clerk signaled that he had something to say to me.

Your predecessor always gave him something extra, he said.

I nodded and was about to give some money to my clerk.

It is better if you give it to him yourself, my clerk said. Meanwhile Mr. Solomon had finished with the book.

That is wonderful, Mr. Solomon, my clerk said. And here is the money.

And here is a little extra, I said quickly, and put my money with the rest.

Mr. Solomon brought his open hand to the place where the peak of his uniform cap must have been thirty years ago. He stuffed the money into a worn wallet. He stood up. I stood and shook his hand. My clerk shook his hand and we both said: Goodbye Mr. Solomon. Mr. Solomon laughed and walked backwards to the door.

Every Wednesday morning the band of the local militia practiced down a back road at a certain distance from my office. With a western wind—and at this time of the year the wind was usually from the west—I could hear bits of music every so often. About two weeks or so after Mr. Solomon's visit I was standing by the window. I could hear that the sounds, usually representing a march, came through more slowly. There was something lugubrious about this music blowing by, something ghostly. A hundred years from now, I thought, someone will stand here and listen to this music and know that it is played by ghosts. By the ghosts of the members of a military band, who are all dead, but who once in a while rise from their graves and meet on the back road to practice for their Last March that will never be held. They are dead. They are all dead. And then I suddenly heard that they were working on Chopin's Funeral March. I went to my clerk.

Do you hear that?, I asked and I raised my finger. My clerk listened.

A funeral march, I said.

Ah, my clerk said, that's right. The King is very sick again. They say that this'll be it.

The King'll be it?, I asked.

He will probably die, my clerk said, resignedly.

Who is the King?, I asked.

Mr. Solomon, of course, my clerk said.

Is Mr. Solomon called a King?, I asked.

Yes, my clerk said. They call him a King in the village, where he lives.

It appeared that Solomon stayed in the village after his retirement, which was unusual. Usually men like Solomon went away. But Solomon had stayed. At sixty years of age he had married a young woman of the island, and because of this had been accepted by the local population as a full-fledged member of the community. As a very valuable member. A man who had seen more of the world than all of them put together, who had considered it a good thing to stay with them and spend his last years in their company. He soon became a kind of oracle and this, in addition to his name, had given him the title of King. King Solomon. And the King was sick and this was going to be it.

What do you mean, this time?, I asked my clerk.

They practice nearly every month for the funeral, my clerk said, and he pointed in the direction of the music.

So he dies almost every month?, I asked.

Yes, my clerk said.

And this time it's going to be it?, I asked.

Yes, my clerk said, but they say that every time.

In the evening I was sitting in front of my house and I saw the doctor passing by.

How's Solomon doing?, I asked.

48

He won't make it through the night, the doctor said.

But the King was still alive the next day and in the beginning of January he came to my office to pick up his pension.

You've been very sick, I believe?, I asked.

The King laughed as exuberantly as was possible for him. He got his money, he got my contribution, and he was off again.

After that, snatches of Chopin would penetrate into my office at various times. They did not sound lugubrious any more. They sounded like the announcement of a contest, of a performance. Ladies and gentlemen, you will now witness the struggle between the King and Death. Once they practiced twice in the same month, but the King was present on the next payday. I gave him double the amount he usually got.

The rest of that month was quiet. On the first day of the next month I had to leave my office at eleven o'clock. I walked into my clerk's office and asked if he needed me for anything.

No, my clerk said. Only, the King hasn't come yet.

That's right, I said, give him a little something from me. And at that same moment we heard the music. The contest music. The music of death.

He won't be coming today, I said.

No, my clerk said.

I went back to my office. I really had to leave, but I hesitated. I called the doctor, but the doctor wasn't home. I was still trying to convince myself that I could easily leave, when my clerk came in with a woman who looked around forty.

This is Mrs. Solomon, he said. Mrs. Solomon has come to pick up her husband's pension. Her husband is sick.

How is he?, I asked.

Oh, Mr. Solomon is very sick, she said.

I showed how sorry I was, and said that we would pay the money. But my clerk hesitated. We left Mrs. Solomon alone for a minute and went to his office. We really cannot do it like that, my clerk said. We can't give it to her, just like that.

Why not?, I asked.

She has to produce proof that he is alive, my clerk said. I thought about that. My clerk was right. From his point of view my clerk was right. If the King was dead at this moment, his pension would stop too. If there was ever a reason for producing an attestation, this was it.[2] It simply was a textbook example of what an attestation was for.

I had an idea. I said to the King's wife: Your husband is sick, and that's why I'll come and visit him. I will come and visit him in an hour, and at the same time I will bring his money.

The King's wife nodded that she understood.

What did she understand? That her husband was King and that another kind of King would be visiting him? That we did not trust things? God knows, maybe she thought it was an excuse and that we did not have enough money on hand. But she left to tell her husband, and I was to follow her an hour later.

When I drove my car into the King's small village, I noticed that she had also told all her husband's subjects. People were standing along the road, and at the house there were so many that I had to walk up to the door between two rows of people. I strode to the door. I actually bowed to the left and to the right, and it seemed as if they were about to cheer.

But inside all was quiet. Cool and quiet, as it is supposed to be in a palace. The King was lying on his bed of state, the square, white bed on which Mr. Solomon lay dying. Lay dying. Because this was going to be it, even I could see that. He had not shut his eyes, but they were covered by a kind of film. He was still alive, but you could not tell that he was still breathing. And there I stood next to his bed with my ledger under my arm. I was standing next to the deathbed of a monarch. In a certain sense I had been a fellow King of his when I walked in, but I was no longer. I had become a subject. Maybe an esteemed subject, maybe a Minister, but still a subject.

I carefully put the book down at the foot of the bed. I thought: It will please him, when he notices it. And if he does not notice it, then it will please him in the place where Kings go when they die. He will laugh about it, the way he laughed in my office. His wife was standing on the other side of the bed. His wife leaned over him and yelled into his ear: The gentleman is here! The gentleman is here to bring you the money!

I saw the King moving. His wife yelled again: The gentleman is here! With the money!

Something stiffened in the face of the King. And I saw that he saw me. I picked up the ledger and held it in front of him, as one would hold a toy in front of a sick child. The King smiled and I laughed also, but it must have been as if I was laughing through tears. I did not say anything, but I pointed to the ledger and I tapped it. I gave his wife the money. I gave his wife all the money I had with me. I even signed the receipt myself. I signed, using the same shaky letters the King used to write his name with, innumerable times, in innumerable ledgers. And I nodded at him. I really should have bowed. A bow for a King who is dying. But I preferred to nod. I nodded warmly at him.

And I went outside to my car between the throngs of waiting people who were mumbling so loudly this time that it could easily have been taken for a suppressed cheer. I was aware of this for the rest of the day. Of this and of the other thing.

The House of the Grandfather

MY boss had called me to announce that too little kapok was being exported.

They're sitting on it, my boss said. They're holding it back. You have to do something about it. I am assigning you the task of checking the supplies and if need be to resort to seizure.

That same afternoon I drove along the big villages of our main island to the harbor to collect supply and export figures. I wrote them down, I added them, I looked at the totals.

This won't do you any good, the harbor master said. You should go see Taronggi III.[1] You should ask him why he won't ship kapok. Taronggi III is the only exporter of importance and he is not exporting. He must have his reasons. Taronggi III knows the market. When Taronggi III doesn't export, then it's better not to export. Why are they bugging us like that?

My boss was not the harbor master's boss, and so I said it would be in the interest of the islands to ship as much kapok as possible at all times.

No one is shipping, said the harbor master. Taronggi III is buying up everything and Taronggi III is biding his time. Why don't you just let him do that.

I think I'll go and see Taronggi III, I said.

Then you will have to wait until tomorrow, the harbor master said. Taronggi III is not available at this hour. He always goes to his new house in the afternoon.

What exactly is this new house?, I asked.

The new house on the road west, the harbor master said. Beyond the big bend.

I thought that that house belonged to one of the islanders, I said.

It is Taronggi III's house, the harbor master said. It was probably built on the land of one of his nephews, but it belongs to Taronggi III.

I decided to give up my kapok investigation for the day. I remembered that it was time I went to see the doctor. At this time of day, the doctor could always be found under the sloping roof in front of his house, with a bottle of rum and as many glasses as there were guests. We were with only two glasses this time.

I am going to see Taronggi III tomorrow, I said.

Taronggi III was Taronggi I's grandson, and Taronggi I was shipwrecked and washed ashore on the big island seventy years ago. Indeed, he was literally washed ashore, tossed through the surf by the waves. He must have drawn himself up as soon as he felt ground under his feet. He must have stood there, dazed, while the water dripped down his body, from his torn shirt, and his tattered pants, as in a painting of a castaway. And the inhabitants of the island must have stood opposite him. There always are people on the beach. There are always people looking at the sea. It must have been very quiet. No one must have said anything. Taronggi did not ask: Have I landed on this or on that island? And the people did not approach him and did not say to him: You are welcome here. We will help you. They must have stood opposite each other in complete silence, and finally Taronggi must have stepped hesitantly away from the water. Hesitant steps through the sucking sand. Steps leading him out of the prison that the water had been for him in the final hours, a prison he had gotten used to. With every step he must have said an increasingly sad farewell to the country he came from. He walked up to the group of men, but they fell back. And then he said something. He said: I was shipwrecked. And the men heard the sound of words in a foreign language. And all of a sudden they all burst out laughing. The shipwrecked man too. Taronggi too. And at that very moment Taronggi became Taronggi I because he never left the island again. For forty years he lived on it, he was married on it, he died on it. Married to a woman from the island. He became somewhat of a potentate, this sailor who was washed ashore, a businessman whose inheritance was so large that the people called his oldest son Taronggi II, out of pure reverence.

Taronggi I reached the age of eighty, Taronggi II became even older, and Taronggi III had to wait forty-five years before he could occupy his father's business throne. Taronggi III was past fifty when his father died. That is the way it is with the Taronggis. The crown princes always reached middle age, and a crown prince had no rights in this family, including no right to his own palace. He had to stay at his father's palace on the big Taronggi estate, even if he was married and had children. It was an estate that was always expanding, until it became a fortress on the edge of the village. Just as the crown prince had to wait until his father died to take over his leadership in business affairs, so too the crown princess had to suffer the domination and in most cases the pestering of her mother-in-law. This was always at the heart of the anecdotes which were told on the island about the Taronggi house: Crown Prince Taronggi who had to ask his father for everything, even the money for his tobacco. But there had never been any sign of protest on the part of the heirs to the throne. They survived their prolonged minority status like mature children, and they took over the reins after the death of their fathers without any change and without a trace of feeling inferior.

Taronggi III is not the worst, the doctor said. But still, he is not as smart as his father. Actually, I knew his father well. Taronggi II taught me to drink rum and I helped him along to the other world. I am going to my grandfather, those were Taronggi II's last words. Those Taronggis have only grandfathers.

Everybody has grandfathers, I said.

Of course, the doctor said, but the Taronggis, understandably enough, dislike their fathers so much that they focus all their family affection on their grandfathers. Including Taronggi II. Taronggi II always spoke about his grandfather. Naturally, he had never known the man, because his grandfather was Taronggi I's father. Taronggi I was the first in the family to come to the island. Taronggi I's father had probably never even heard of our islands and certainly not of the grandchild he had here. But if you heard Taronggi II, you'd think that he had sat on his grandfather's knee or played pool with him in a café in Tarragona. You know that Taronggi I came from Tarragona. He was probably a sailor when his ship sank off the coast here. Well, Taronggi II knew everything about Tarragona. He never denied it when people, unfamiliar with the history of the Taronggis, asked him if he had spent his youth in Tarragona. I remember that there was a merchant here once who actually did come from Tarragona. I am sure that man never did such good business in all his life as with Taronggi II. Taronggi II was practically giving his kapok away only because of his love for Tarragona.

Is Taronggi III also crazy about this great-grandfather?, I asked.

Taronggi III is crazy about his own grandfather, about Taronggi I, the doctor said.

That's really too bad, I said.

Taronggi III fantasized quite a story about Taronggi I, the doctor said. Taronggi III says his grandfather was a rich young man, the son of a shipowner from Tarragona, and that he jumped overboard off the coast here, because he thought the island was so beautiful. Taronggi III says that Taronggi I had been given a magnificent house in Tarragona by his father, but, Taronggi III says, Taronggi I loved the people of the islands so much that he never wanted to leave them again, despite the beautiful house. Taronggi III even has a painting of the house in Tarragona.

How did he get that?, I asked.

One time Taronggi III received a postcard with a house on it. Printed at the bottom was: Casa de this or that and then Tarragona. Taronggi III did not rest until he knew that casa means house, and from that point on the house was the one that belonged to his grandfather in Tarragona. He even had it copied. An exceptionally bad painting.

I could give it a try by beginning the conversation with Tarragona, I said.

Do you need kapok?, the doctor asked.

My boss wants to know why no kapok is being exported, I said.

You should ask Taronggi III about his new house, the doctor said.

The new house right by the curve in the road heading west?, I asked.

It is his grandfather's house, the doctor said. He had it built according to the picture on the postcard.

The next morning I drove to the Taronggi estate. A shy young man, presumably Taronggi IV, told me that Taronggi III was in his office and he even took me to it but he did not go in with me. Taronggi III was sitting at his desk, rocking in an easy chair.

I have come for a little visit, I said.

What would you like to drink?, Taronggi III asked.

A cup of coffee, please, I said.

The coffee was brought in by a shy young woman.

My oldest daughter-in-law, Taronggi III said, not unfriendly. I made a bow to the crown princess.

She helps my wife, Taronggi III said. The crown princess laughed, but still just as shyly.

I am here about the kapok, I said.

Ha, ha, ha, Taronggi III laughed.

My boss is afraid that not enough kapok is being exported, I said.

Ha, ha, ha, Taronggi III laughed. Hanging behind the desk was a large painting of a man in a kind of pirate costume. He wore a smooth red scarf knotted around his head and golden earrings. Taronggi III saw me looking at the painting.

My grandfather, he said, from Tarragona.

I thought, I can't say that I have been in Tarragona once. According to the doctor, that would have been the way to do business with Taronggi II, but matters could be different with Taronggi III. Taronggi III had never been to Tarragona himself and he might think it unpleasant if someone, recently arrived on the islands, knew more about his country of origin than he did. So I said: I have heard that your family stems from Tarragona. I felt very satisfied with the "stems" and Taronggi III did too. Taronggi III laughed: Ha, ha, ha!

I said: Your grandfather can't have been a sailor.

Merchant, Taronggi III said. Merchant and shipowner.

Your grandfather must have traded in kapok also, I said.

Ha, ha, ha, Taronggi III laughed.

Is the price of kapok going up soon?, I asked.

That is difficult to say, Taronggi III said. Some people expect it to rise and others to fall. There is no way to tell.

Will you be buying a lot more kapok?, I asked. We would really appreciate your letting us know, my boss and I.

56

The question is if it's still worth the trouble to buy up more kapok, Taronggi III said.

I have been in Tarragona, I said. I have been in Tarragona many times. I know the city very well.

That's wonderful, Taronggi III said. Then you must come and see my grandfather's house. My grandfather had a house in Tarragona. As the son of a shipowner, he had a very beautiful house in Tarragona. I had it copied. You must see it. You must come and see it right now. I usually only go there in the afternoon, but I will show it to you right now. And Taronggi III jumped up from behind his desk, walked to the door, and yelled: Car! Moments later, there was a car in front of the office. Taronggi III opened the door for me, got in himself, and off we went, on the road heading west. The house was just outside the village, near the curve. We stopped by the side of the road.

We'll just take a look at the house from the outside, Taronggi III said. You should know that the house is completely empty inside. It has not been furnished yet.

You aren't storing kapok in it, are you?, I asked.

Ha, ha, ha!, Taronggi III laughed.

It was a huge, low white house with pillars in front and at the back. The windows were open and the rooms were indeed completely empty.

I always come here alone, Taronggi III said. I come here alone, almost every afternoon. But for you I'm making an exception. You have been in Tarragona. Did I build correctly? Is there something you would like to change?

I think it is a magnificent house, I said. It is exactly like the houses in Tarragona.

Just tell me if you want something changed, Taronggi III said.

It is just right like that, I said.

Any change you think necessary, Taronggi III said.

I will tell my boss that there is nothing going on in kapok at the moment, I said.

Any change you think necessary, Taronggi III said. And any change your boss thinks necessary.

The Meal

M R. ZEINAL stood on a big sheet of paper in the front room of his house.[1] The paper was at least ten feet long and six feet wide and it was completely covered with small letters.

This is my family tree, Mr. Zeinal said.

I took my shoes off and stood next to Mr. Zeinal on the sheet of paper.

Here are my great-grandfather's eighty-four children, Mr. Zeinal said, and he pointed to a long list of names connected to a single name by a brace. We stooped. We knelt down. We crawled along the paper. We followed the eighty-four children through life and death. It was very interesting. Is the Prince on it?, I asked. I knew that Mr. Zeinal had a distant relative who was a Prince.

The Prince has a different lineage, Mr. Zeinal said. The Prince and I are related in the female line only.

I knew that Mr. Zeinal considered his own descent more distinguished than that of the Prince. I said: The Prince has a magnificent house, though.

The Prince has three houses, Mr. Zeinal said obligingly. Two on this island and one on a small island near the bay on the east coast. All three are very beautiful. Very beautiful and very old. You really should have a look at the Prince's houses.

I said I only knew the house to the west of the town, about six miles away.

That is the Prince's country house, Mr. Zeinal said. Very nice, but the house here on the village square is nicer. Old and very curious.

I said: But which house is that? I thought I knew all the houses on the village square.

You cannot see it from the square, Mr. Zeinal said. There are too many trees in front of it.

I would certainly like to have a look at it sometime, I said.

I will arrange it for you, Mr. Zeinal said.

The next morning I received a note from Mr. Zeinal, inviting me for a visit to the Prince's house. We were to have dinner there. The Prince would very much appreciate it, Mr. Zeinal wrote. I will come and pick you up in an hour.

I am going to be picked up by Mr. Zeinal in one hour, to go and have a look at the Prince's house and to eat there, I said to my clerk. My clerk made a polite bow, actually more in the direction of the still absent Mr. Zeinal than in my direction.

It is very nice of Mr. Zeinal to invite me, I said. I am pleased.

Mr. Zeinal is a relative of mine, my clerk said.

Then I certainly must have seen your name on his family tree, I said. Just yesterday I saw Mr. Zeinal's family tree. And so you are also a relative of the Prince. I heard from Mr. Zeinal that the Prince has three houses. This morning we are going to the house on the village square.

That's the bird house, my clerk said.

I asked: Why the bird house?

There are birds living in it, my clerk said.

Does the Prince also live there?, I asked. That is difficult to say, my clerk said. The Prince lives sometimes here and sometimes there.

I have never seen the Prince, I said. Do you think he will be home when Mr. Zeinal and I will pay our visit?

That's difficult to say, my clerk said. The Prince is very old. I don't think he receives very many guests any more.

Only a few people on the island have actually seen the Prince, I said. The doctor has never seen him and the harbor master hasn't either. Only Mr. Taronggi has seen him at one time or another.

Mr. Taronggi's father used to do business with the Prince, my clerk said.

Of course, Mr. Zeinal must see the Prince often, I said.

Of course, my clerk said. Mr. Zeinal always sees a lot more than other people.

I knew that the people on the island believed Mr. Zeinal had miraculous powers. The people believed that he could perform magic. I had once seen him perform his magic. We had both been visiting the district chief, and had gone on to a small cemetery behind the district chief's house. There was a small garden house in the cemetery grounds and we went inside, Mr. Zeinal, the district chief, and I. We saw a stone coffin standing on the ground.

One of my ancestors, Mr. Zeinal had said, pointing to the coffin. He had picked a green leaf from a shrub, and he put it on the casket while mumbling something.[2]

Later he told us that it had been a magic formula. I have linked my fate to that of the leaf, he said. As long as the leaf stays there, I stay the same as I am now.

I thought that I better not ask my clerk if Mr. Zeinal had linked his fate to that of the Prince. If he, while standing across from the Prince, had mumbled a magic formula which would have tied the Prince to Mr. Zeinal's life like a shadow. While I was thinking this, a car stopped in front of my office and Mr. Zeinal got out, after which we both got in again and drove to the Prince's house.

From the square the house was indeed not visible because of the tall trees in front of it. The trees were big and leafy, and it seemed as if we were suddenly walking from the village square with its glaring light into a small dark forest. A very small forest, because it was only fifty yards to the entrance of the house. I told Mr. Zeinal that there were fairy tales about houses and palaces hidden in dark forests. Mr. Zeinal did not find this difficult to believe.

There is a fairy tale about this house of the Prince, he said. I will tell it to you during dinner.

The car stopped under the trees, right near the entrance of the house. I noticed that the branches touched the house. While we were getting out, a man stealthily walked by, bowing deeply. We walked up the three steps to the entrance, and he opened the door for us. He was a poorly dressed man.

We will go inside now, Mr. Zeinal said. You can shake the hand of the man who opened the door for us. He is a poor relation of the Prince.

I shook the man's hand and we went inside. It must have been a large hall where we entered, but it was impossible to make out at first, because it was completely dark. A sickly sweet smell met us, and I heard a fluttering above me as though hundreds of birds were flying along the ceiling. On the floor was a thick carpet, thick enough to make our feet sink in it. I remembered that my clerk had called this house a bird house, and I said to Mr. Zeinal: It seems there are birds here.

Very many birds, Mr. Zeinal said. The Prince lets a lot of birds nest in this room. They come in through the openings beneath the roof tiles. The Prince sells their dung.

Their dung?, I asked.

The dung. We are walking on it, Mr. Zeinal said.

I actually thought we were walking on a thick carpet, I said.

It is very dry, the dung, Mr. Zeinal said. It won't make us dirty. Only a bit dusty. The Prince sells it once a year. I think it's already sixteen inches thick. The Prince will probably sell it next month. We'll now go to the back of the house. There are no birds there.

I had gotten used to the dark. I saw a hazy figure in front of me, and a little later even a shaft of light came in. The poor relation had opened a door at the back of the hall. I looked up. I saw the birds flying around. There were, indeed, surprisingly many.

We entered the next room. It was much lighter. It contained a large square bench, a good six feet long and six feet wide, with a couple of greasy pillows on it. I got the impression that this was where the poor relation slept, and I said so to Mr. Zeinal.

Why, certainly, Mr. Zeinal said. This used to be the room of the Prince's wife, and the large hall that we just walked through was the reception room.

I bet there were no birds in those days, I said.

That's right, Mr. Zeinal said. I'll tell you a story about this women's room during dinner.

Are we going to eat here?, I asked.

We are eating on the porch in back, Mr. Zeinal said.

Is the Prince waiting for us there?, I asked.

The Prince?, Mr. Zeinal asked. No, the Prince won't be there. The Prince is very old.

Does the Prince still live here?, I asked.

The Prince now lives here and then somewhere else, Mr. Zeinal said.

Does the Prince know that I will be dining here today?, I asked.

Certainly, Mr. Zeinal said.

Meanwhile the poor relation had opened a door in the back wall of the women's room, and going through it, we came out on the porch at the back of the house. Here the trees were not as close to the house as in front. I saw a small brick oven under one of the trees. There was a fire in it, and there was a man standing near it, just as poorly dressed as the poor relation. The poor relation walked over to him. Mr. Zeinal said: Let's sit down.

I noticed that a table was set on the open porch. With two chairs. I understood that the poor relation would not be eating with us. He was to be more our maître d'hôtel. He waited until Mr. Zeinal and I were seated, and then he busily started to berate the man by the oven.

The man by the oven is certainly not a relative of the Prince, I said.

Oh no, Mr. Zeinal said.

He is the Prince's cook, of course, I said.

That's right, Mr. Zeinal said.

You could even say that he was an excellent cook. He had made us a delicious aromatic soup with big chunks of meat floating in it. These chunks of meat were scooped up out of our plates by the poor relation and placed on a plate next to our soup plates. The meat was very tasty and not overcooked.

I announced that I had seldom tasted such delicious soup and such good meat. I said: I have eaten well in any number of places all around the world, but I don't think that the soup and meat were ever any better. You can tell this soup has been prepared for a Prince. I mean, of course, I said hurriedly, for the table of a Prince, because the Prince himself is not eating with us.

At that point I thought I heard a giggle behind us in the house. I looked at Mr. Zeinal, but he was quietly cutting his meat into small pieces. He said: I promised you that I would tell you a story. The story about the women's room. It must have happened around the time the first ancestor of the Prince arrived on the island and built his palace here. The women's room is the only part of this old palace that has been preserved. The present house has been built around it.

When the first ancestor of the Prince arrived on the island, he had to wage war against the ruling Prince at the time, and to pester the ruling Prince a little, the ancestor of our Prince made a vow that he would deflower all the young women of the island in one night.

I said: Boy-o-boy!

Mr. Zeinal laughed heartily. He said: It is a fairy tale, of course, but it is said that the ancestor of our Prince was true to his vow, except for one young girl. She was the daughter of the ruling Prince, who wasn't really ruling anymore. This daughter was a sorceress, and she flew through the air to this part of the island and kept herself hidden here.

She was so beautiful, though, that her hiding place did not remain a secret for very long, and the ancestor of our Prince pursued her and tracked her down. But at the moment he entered her house, she used her magic to change herself into a senile old man. Naturally, the ancestor of our Prince became terribly angry. He took her with him and locked her up in the palace he had built here. Once he had locked the door of her room, she turned again into a beautiful young woman, and she'd stick her head out the window and laugh at the ancestor of the Prince, who got terribly angry and went inside again. But as soon as he was inside, he saw nothing but a giggling old man. It seems this continued for a while, but in the end they reached an agreement and the ancestor of the Prince made the sorceress his first consort. After that they got along very well together, although it seems that the sorceress would change herself into an old man every once in a while.

And her spirit returns here every so often, I said.

I don't think so, Mr. Zeinal said.

It may be a coincidence, I said, but just now, I thought I heard an old man giggling behind us.

And at the moment I said this, I heard it again.

It is probably your imagination, Mr. Zeinal said.

I think so too, I said.

It often happens, Mr. Zeinal said, that people imagine such things when they hear old stories.

I am more than willing to believe it, I said. The giggling was almost continuous now.

The meal came to an end. Mr. Zeinal and I both stood up. I

thanked the poor relation and I thanked the cook. I said to Mr. Zeinal: I have appreciated this visit and this meal very much.

It will please the Prince very much to hear this, Mr. Zeinal said.
The Prince always takes pleasure in receiving guests.

That befits a Prince, I said.

The Swamp

TOWARD the afternoon I arrived in Naman's village, but the people there told me that Naman had moved six miles farther. Behind the swamp, they said.

And how do I get through the swamp?, I asked.

Well, there were two roads, a high road and a low road. The high road was a detour.

A detour?, I asked uncertainly.

The low road is not passable at high tide, a man said.

And is it low tide now?, I asked.

The water was going down already. If I wanted to wait an hour, it would work.

In my thoughts I saw a slippery path with slippery tree roots sticking out on all sides. Tree roots like snakes. I asked: How much of a detour is the high road?

An hour, the same man said cautiously.

Walking an hour longer. Walking even more. When did that damned Naman move behind the swamp?

Why doesn't Mr. Naman live in the village anymore?, I asked.

Mr. Naman had a house built behind the swamp, the man who was speaker for the group said.

But why behind the swamp?, I asked again.

Everyone was silent. Even the man who had been speaking up to now. Finally one of them said helplessly: Mr. Naman wanted to build a house behind the swamp.

Is it a nice house?, I asked quickly.

Oh yes, the house was nice, it was very nice. A lot of hard work was put into getting the lumber to the other side of the swamp.

I would really like to have something to eat, I said. They took me to a house that turned out to be the house of the man who did the talking.

Three hours later he and I were on our way. I should have left sooner, of course, but only after I sat down and ate did it really hit me how tired I was from walking the entire morning.

So we are taking the low road, I said. My host, who was going to be my guide, nodded. It was a wide road and not as soggy as I had imagined. A lot of people must take this path, I said to my guide.

A lot of people had followed this path lately with lumber for Mr. Naman.

How long has the house been finished?, I asked.

A month ago they had taken the last of the lumber.

We had already been walking more than an hour and the path was still dry. It did not look at all as if it was regularly under water. There also was not much to be seen of the swamp. It could only be smelled, the swamp. A stifling stuffiness from brackish water and rotting plants.

How high does the water get here at high tide?, I asked.

Oh, the tide does not rise that much, my guide said.

I did not say anything. I understood that we were on the high road. I had lost my chance of taking the low road because of my dawdling. Finally, we came to a crossroads and my guide stood still.

If you want, he said, we can leave the path here. It is a little wet, but it is not bad and it is much shorter.

I said, all right, and a bit later we were sopping in the water up to our ankles. In invisible water. No water was to be seen anywhere; there were only gray bushes with pale green leaves which we passed, and entangled plants that we stepped on. My guide advanced with big sure steps and I followed him as well as I could. I lifted my legs high every time, just as he did, to avoid tripping over the roots which I felt constantly under my feet.

After a half hour, up to my knees stiff with mud, I arrived at a small open plain, and at the end of this plain stood a house. A big white house under the evening sun, with a roofed terrace in front. It was a wonderful sight after all those gray swamp bushes. Naman was really an exceptional fellow, after all. We walked toward it.

I paid, thanked my guide, and stumbled onto the terrace. I was tired. I sat down on one of the large chairs standing there. Naman would appear soon. Naman would come to give me something to drink. He had always been an exceptionally attentive host.

But I did not hear anything. I started calling: "Hey! hey!"

But no one appeared.

My guide had gone on to the back of the house and returned to say goodbye. He wanted to get home before dark.

And this time you'll take the low road, I'm sure, I said, and laughed.

My guide also laughed.

Was Mr. Naman at the back of the house?, I asked.

Mr. Naman is coming, my guide said. He said goodbye to me once more and left. I watched him walk across the plain until he disappeared into the swamp. Then I heard voices behind me in the house. I recognized Naman's voice. Naman always had a somewhat cool, authoritarian manner of speech. Most of his colleagues from the service said that Naman was a conceited fool. Naman was a go-getter. But I had always known that it wasn't true. Naman was a good person, an honest person, and in a certain sense even cordial. But his cordiality was exceptional. His cordiality was stylized. Naman had one big ambition in life. He wanted to be considerate. He wanted to be the most considerate of men. "The fast chair-getter" and "the walking cigarette lighter," they had called him at one of his posts, where Naman had lived for a year. It had given him a bad name with the men, but this was totally unfair. Naman did his small favors not to build up his career, unless he saw his career as the career of a courteous person. The means were not means to him, but the end.

There had also been a girl. Rie Winters. Maria Winters, Naman had always called her. He worked pretty hard on her. One evening, a month after Naman had been transferred, a rather drunken evening, she told us about it, choking with laughter. She wouldn't have minded fooling around a little, she told us, but Naman handed her cigarettes and Naman lit them and Naman got her something to drink, and Naman asked her if she was cold.

And when I said yes, he went to get my coat, she'd shrieked. And we all howled with laughter, and this story of typical Naman considerateness became the cause for an uncommonly crude evening.

I heard steps in back of me and I turned around. In the open doorway of his house stood Naman, his right arm around a shotgun.

Look who's here, Naman said.

Hello Naman, I said, and I stood up and walked toward him. I thought it was time for a visit.

Well, that's fine, Naman said. An excellent idea. A friendly idea. That was exactly like Naman, the opinionated, considerate Naman, who felt he had to make his guests feel at ease. We shook each other's hand. Naman rested his gun against the side of the house and called out to his servant to bring us a couple of bottles of beer. The beer was nicely cold. Just like Naman. Naturally, there wasn't an ice cube to be had in the general area, but Naman provided a cold glass of beer. I was glad I had come. I asked: Naman, why did you go and live behind the swamp? Or is there a village behind this house?

Behind the house?, Naman asked, astonished and almost frightened. A village behind this house? Not at all, what makes you think so? Behind the house is the swamp, and next to the house is the swamp. This is a small island in the swamp. Interesting, huh?

Yes, I said, you are quite right. Naman always imparted some of his attentiveness to his surroundings, at least if you were alone with him. He lifted you, as it were, to his own level of politeness. If I had come to visit him with somebody else, we would have spoken roughly to Naman about the insanity of living alone on a small island in the middle of the swamp. But I was alone and so I said: Yes. And I said: It must give you a feeling of, how shall I put it, of noble solitude.

Indeed, Naman said. Of course, this was the way to talk to Naman when you were alone with him.

There is a kind of ridge that is never covered by water, Naman said, except during the spring tide.

That must be the path I took, I said.

Undoubtedly, Naman said.

I asked: Why have you come to live here, Naman?

It was, of course, very stupid to ask something like that, after I had just spoken of noble solitude, but Naman gave an answer.

Naman always gave an answer when asked something.

There was no one in the village to be with, Naman said. I mean, no one to talk to.

I see, I said.

There was no one to talk to in the village, and that's why Naman lived on an island in a swamp, where there was absolutely no one to talk to, where he saw absolutely nobody. Maybe it wasn't all that crazy. Perhaps it was less bad to be alone than to live in a village where there was no one to talk to.

In any case, it seems like a nice house, I said. Obligingly, Naman got up in order to show me around.

But it wasn't a nice house at all. From the outside it had seemed to have something, but inside it was just awful. Three elongated rooms along the entire width of the house, one after the other. The walls were painted red, and our footsteps sounded dull on the wooden floor.

Maybe a bit dark inside, I said. Maybe it would have been better if you had chosen a lighter color, although it's easy on the eyes like this.

Naman laughed a little shyly. To tell you the truth, there was no other paint. You don't have to be afraid to say it's ugly. I also think it's very ugly. A dirty color.

We sat outside again. Naman pushed another bottle of beer toward me. The sound of the beer in the glass was the only sound in the silence. The sun had set. The sun had disappeared behind the swamp.

Next time I'll bring some paint, I said. That would be extremely nice of you, Naman said. He stood up and began to walk back and forth on the porch.

Every time he walked away from me and I was looking at his back, I saw him quickly nod his head a few times. Once I even thought I heard him mumble something to himself. I asked: Say Naman, how do you get light around here?

Huh?, Naman asked, confused. He was walking away from me at that moment, and I had apparently disturbed him between a few nods.

It isn't dark yet, he said. It isn't that dark yet, he shouted once more.

No, not at all, I said, it isn't that dark yet.

Petroleum, Naman said. You would like a drink, wouldn't you? Ha ha, of course you would like a drink, with all this talk about darkness.

He stopped walking back and forth. He came and stood next to my chair.

Candles too, he said. But only petroleum out here on the porch. In the evening it's too windy here for candles. It had indeed become a bit windy. And the wind brought the stench of the swamp. The stifling odor I had smelled this afternoon when I walked through it was now rolling, as it were, toward the house.

It is becoming dark after all, Naman said. It always gets dark so darn fast around here. Why on earth didn't you come a little earlier?

He rubbed his head a few times.

I am going to get a drink, he then said.

He walked inside the house and slammed the door behind him.

I heard the sound of his footsteps in the front room. Afterwards another door slammed shut and everything became silent. Naman did not come back. A bit later an older man, Naman's servant, brought a lamp, a bottle of gin, and two glasses. I asked him where Naman was. Mr. Naman was changing.

I asked the servant if they had a lot of visitors here. No, actually there never were any visitors. It was too far and too difficult to come through the swamp.

I asked: Does the swamp always stink like this? The swamp only stank in the evening after sunset. In the morning the air was clean again.

How's it going, Naman?, I called to the back. There was no answer. I've started already!, I called out. I did not get an answer. It had gradually become completely dark and very quiet everywhere, in the house too, especially in the house. Was it because of the silence that I walked on tiptoe to the door in the front wall and which I opened a crack to peek inside, in order to see where Naman was?

Naman was standing in the room with his back to the wall. The door was in the corner and I saw him from the side. He was shaking his head, at first slowly, then more and more violently. He muttered: No, no! He turned in my direction. I jumped a few steps away from the door. I acted as though I was staring into the vague darkness of the swamp. I heard Naman laugh in back of me. I didn't hear a door, but I considered the possibility that Naman would be able to open the door without a sound and that he could be standing right behind me. I turned around, but there was no one. I went back to the table and poured myself another glass of gin. I heard Naman call his servant. Shortly afterwards a woman came out to the terrace from the back. She was carrying a crystal decanter on a tray. She put the decanter on the table and poured the gin into it from the crock. I asked her if she was the wife of the servant. She said: Yes. She apparently thought that I wanted to know where her husband was, and she said: My husband is looking for flowers for Mr. Naman.

I asked: Do flowers grow here? Yes, flowers grew in some places in between the roots of the swamp bushes.

I held the decanter up to the light. The decanter sparkled in the yellow light of the petroleum lamp. A flower in the swamp. I heard clattering in the house, but Naman stayed away. I went back to the door and looked through the crack. Naman was not in the front room and I did not hear him talking or laughing. When I turned around, I saw someone standing by the table. It was Naman's servant bringing a second decanter.

Find any flowers?, I asked. Yes, the flowers had been found.

What's taking Mr. Naman so long?, I asked. Mr. Naman was changing.

I unscrewed the stopper of the second decanter and smelled it. Sherry, I said. I filled my glass half full and drank. It was sherry.

Does Mr. Naman drink sherry nowadays?, I asked, but the servant had vanished.

Everybody keeps on vanishing around here, I said. I called: Naman, the sherry is getting warm. There was no answer. Later I forgot about the sherry. I called: Naman, if you don't come out pretty soon, the gin will be all gone. Is the crock really empty already?, I said to myself as I held the decanter with the gin up to the light of the lamp. The decanter sparkled in the light of the petroleum lamp, and behind it I saw something black. After I had put the decanter down, I saw it was Naman. Naman in a tuxedo, with a sparkling white shirt, a black bow tie, and a red flower in his buttonhole.

He stayed beside the table and poured himself a glass of sherry, and finished it in one gulp. At first I thought: Well, it's not that strange that a girl wanted to fool around with him. He doesn't look half-bad like that, this Naman. I said: I hope you don't mind, Naman, if I stay like this, and I pointed to my pants which were still gray from the mud.

Naman looked at me proudly and contemptuously, and said curtly: Yes, I mind very much.

He picked up the decanter of sherry by the neck and walked away, going inside. I thought: I will have one more glass of gin and then I will also go inside. I called: Naman, are we going to have a bite to eat? There was no answer. A little later I went inside. There was no one in the front room. I opened the door of the second room.

In the middle of the second room was a table covered with a white tablecloth on which candles were burning. There were red flowers on the white tablecloth, there were sparkling glasses and a bottle of wine. Naman was sitting at the table, and I saw that it had been set for three people. I sat down at one of the empty places, and I heard Naman say softly: Don't pay too much attention to him, Maria. He is a bit drunk.

The servant brought us soup. I said: Ah, soup! and I started eating. When I was finished, I saw that Naman's plate was still half full. He talked in the direction of the third chair. I heard him ask: Are you sure you aren't too warm, Maria, with all the windows shut?

I saw that there was no soup in Maria's plate. I said: It's stifling in here. Naman motioned peremptorily for me to be quiet, but a little later he stood up and opened the windows to let some air in.

After the soup plates had been taken away, Naman poured the wine. The attentive Naman, I thought. First a little in his own glass, then a glass for Maria, and then more for himself. Afterwards he shoved the bottle in my direction, without looking at me.

The soup had been delicious and the wine was delicious, but the rest of the meal was terrible. The meat was bad and the vegetables were bad and the potatoes weren't there, luckily enough, because they doubtlessly would have been exceptionally bad. I noticed that the third plate did not get anything but a glass of wine. I said: Maria doesn't eat very much.

I forbid you to say Maria!, Naman screamed.

The wine is delicious, though, I said quickly, and I filled my glass again. I noticed that I would have a difficult time keeping up with Naman. Naman drank one glass after another. When the bottle was empty, the servant came with a new one. We sat. Naman and I drank our wine. Naman talked courteously to Maria, and I sat and listened or I did not listen. I stopped listening from the moment I had become very sad. I said: Naman! Naman! Listen! Listen you two, Naman and Maria!

Naman was facing the third chair and was resting his left elbow on the tablecloth. He was holding his glass of wine in his right hand.

I yelled: Naman, it is dangerous! You shouldn't lean your elbow on the tablecloth like that. It is dangerous. Maria is doing the same. It rests on the swamp, only on the swamp, and you are sinking right through it. Look—and I pointed at the wine stains—it is already coming through. It is treacherous, the swamp. You two are sinking through it. With your elbows.

I pushed away from the table. I did not dare lean on it myself anymore. I looked around. I saw a tray in a corner of the room. I got the tray. I walked over to it carefully, lifting my legs up high so as not to trip in the swamp. I put the tray down in front of me on the tablecloth. A bottle fell, a glass broke, but I knew that I wouldn't sink into the swamp when I rested my head on my arms on top of the tray.

When I woke up, Naman was sitting next to me at the table. He was staring in front of him. I couldn't speak because of my dry mouth. I got up and walked to the corner where the bottles were. The bottles were empty. I went back to the table. There wasn't a bottle on the table anymore. Only Maria's full glass was still there. I looked at Naman. Naman kept on looking straight ahead of him. I poured half of the wine out of Maria's glass into Naman's glass. I said: Here Naman, and I drank the other half myself. Naman looked up when I gave him the wine. He said: Thank you, and he drank his half.

I said: What time is it? It's getting quite cool.

It must be almost morning, Naman said.

We got up and went outside. It was indeed getting light. I noticed that something was standing against the wall of the porch. It was Naman's gun. The barrel was wet with dew.

I said: That's not very good for it, and Naman said: That stupid servant forgot to take it inside again.

Before us ribbons of mist were moving across the open space in front of the house. Ribbons of mist? Did I see a white figure hurrying away in the direction of the swamp? Oh no.

The Thief

I DID not know Horan before I had him put in jail. Horan lived in one of the tiny villages close to the north coast, but far enough from the sea not to want to be a fisherman. Horan was a cattleman and his neighbor was a cattleman, and Horan had stolen a bull calf from his neighbor in broad daylight. He had gone to his neighbor's cowshed with a rope at 2:00 P.M. and had opened the door and taken the calf. There were never many people around at that time of day. It was much too hot to be out at two o'clock in the afternoon. That day it had been so hot that the quivering of the air was almost audible. And in that quivering air Horan had walked from his neighbor's cowshed to his own cowshed with the bull calf behind him on a rope. But he had been seen. One of the other neighbors had been dozing under the little sloping roof behind his house, and he had seen Horan pass by with the calf. The neighbor was instantly wide awake. He understood immediately what was going on. He did not say anything, did not yell. He waited until Horan had disappeared into his own cowshed, and after that he went to the neighbor who owned the bull calf and told him everything.

The neighbor who owned the calf, and the neighbor who had seen everything, had gone to the cowshed together and had found it empty.

We have to go to the police, they had said to one another, and that was what they did. There was one police officer in the village. He had been sleeping under the sloping roof of his office. They had awakened him and the three of them had gone to Horan's cowshed. The

75

door was open and inside they saw Horan and the bull calf, and Horan had just fetched a bucket of water to let the calf drink.

A month later it was the turn of Horan's village for a court session. The clerk of the court and I sat behind a long table on an open gallery in front of the district chief's house. The people of the village sat and stood in a half-circle in front of us in the yard. The police officer of the village was there, as well as a policeman we had brought from the capital. The clerk of the court read out the name of the accused and the policeman from the capital yelled: Come on! and the policeman from the village pushed the accused, and the accused stumbled into the center of the circle where he sat down on the ground, and the on-lookers grinned and when once in a while the pushing was a little too forceful the accused would also grin and we, behind the table, would grin too in order to make up for it.

In this manner the clerk and I had fined or put in detention about forty accused. Then Horan's case came up. The policeman from the capital again yelled: Come on! but this time the policeman from the village didn't push. He grabbed Horan by the arm and led him before his judges. Horan sat down and the policeman stood next to him.

The clerk of the court said that Horan was accused of having stolen a bull calf and he called upon the policeman to bear witness. The policeman declared that he had been awakened during the afternoon in question by Horan's neighbors and that the three of them had gone to Horan's yard and that they had found the calf in Horan's cowshed at the very moment when Horan was giving the calf a drink from a bucket of water and that he, the officer, had confiscated the calf and the bucket.

I asked: How confiscated?

It appeared that the policeman had taken the calf and the bucket to his own house. He had fed and watered the calf all the time up to the court session, and he had it with him now.

I asked: Why was the calf confiscated?

The policeman said that the calf was a piece of evidence. He said: I have brought the calf as evidence for your worships.

I asked the clerk of the court: Does he mean the calf is here?

Yes, said the clerk of the court.

So where is it?, I asked.

It is next door in the district chief's barn, the policeman said.

We'll have a look at it then, I said to the clerk of the court.

I think the policeman will appreciate that, said the clerk of the court.

We got up from behind our table and we walked over to the district chief's small shed, the clerk of the court and I walking ahead of the others, with the policeman directly next to us to show us the way. Behind us came the district chief and the district chief's deputy, the owner of the bull calf, and the witness who had seen Horan, and Horan himself followed them. Trailing behind was a parade of villagers.

The light in the small shed was dim. The calf stood beside a wall in a bed of hay. It had soft brown hair with a few white spots but the head was an even brown. It had a bucket of water and a trough filled with sliced turnips. The turnips looked quite delicious. The six of us stood around the calf. Myself, the clerk of court, the district chief, the policeman, the owner, and the thief. Horan, the thief, stood next to me, right in front of the calf's head.

How old is it?, I asked.

Six months, Horan said.

The animal was only six months old and already his eyes were pools of sadness.

It is a beautiful animal, I said.

It is a fat little fellow, Horan said. It is a beautiful little thing. And he slapped the animal on the flank.

This is the bucket, the policeman said.

What bucket?, I asked.

The piece of evidence, said the policeman.

I'm sending it to the fair in the capital next year, the owner said.

He is bound to win first prize, Horan said.

Well, let's go back, I said.

When we were sitting behind the table again, I asked the clerk of court: What's the penalty for this?

We could give him six months, the clerk of courts said. But the minimum penalty is much less.

What is the minimum penalty?, I asked.

One month, the clerk of court said.

Two months, I said.

Two months!, shouted the clerk of court. And the evidence went back to the owner.

After the session we had a cup of coffee at the district chief's. We went home in the car. On the way back we passed Horan. He had rented a cart along with three other convicts for the ride to the jail. It was twelve miles and on the way they would certainly stop to eat somewhere. They probably would not reach the jail before nightfall.

When they saw my car, they pulled over. They greeted us. We returned their greetings, the clerk of court and I.

The Hunt

CAPTAIN Florines was a rebel.[1] Perhaps he himself did not even know why. And I, who as an official was on the side of the government, I had no idea. At least not in the beginning. Toward the end of the hunt, when I could hardly tell him, myself, and the wild boar apart, I think I understood why Florines lived that way and why he had to die that way. Or perhaps not. I don't know.

The shape Florines first gave to his rebellion seemed to be the usual one for our district. I remember hearing the first message about it on a Monday night and feeling that I had to say—and maybe did say—damn it, another one of these annoying idiots who's gone berserk. For they always went berserk, those rebels, and not a little, either. They thought of themselves as little Messiahs, and the millenniums they offered were restricted to very small areas, where the inhabitants no longer would have to pay taxes.[2] They gathered a number of disciples around them, they usually put on white clothes, and they fought until they died. There never was a happy ending to their revolts. Hence sufficient reason to have someone say, damn it, when he hears on a Monday morning that such a revolt has broken out in his district.

Further reports about the event came in slowly and incompletely. First, rumors that two villages had been burned down. I simply refused to believe this. Rebels of the little Messiah category never burned down villages.

They never burn down villages, I said to my clerk.

No, my clerk said, but he said it uncertainly.

At two o'clock my superior telephoned from the capital to ask me why the hell I hadn't done anything yet, and that two villages had been burned down. I replied I was waiting for further reports and that the burning of those two villages was hogwash, they never did anything like that. You know that yourself, don't you, I said, indirectly appealing to his vast experience of many years, for the man was always very sensitive about that. I added: Those two villages are still there, the way they were yesterday and the way they were the day before. Well, he agreed to forget about the burned villages. But you must go there, he said. You must restore order this very day.

The man was quite right. Order had to be restored and I had to do that, and I could only do that by going there. But after I hung up, I noticed that it was still two o'clock and on any other day that meant going home, eating, taking a bath, and having a siesta. And I started cursing myself for my laziness that morning. If only I had gone out that morning, I could have had him behind bars by now, this Captain Florines. Damn it, I said to myself, Captain Florines? That is Florines, of course. How is it possible, for Christ's sake.

Florines, the conceited little hunter, the flunky of other wealthier hunters. Florines, who shot wild boars and sold the dead animals to butchers. Florines, who organized hunting parties for money and fancy talk, and who—if you wanted to believe the gossip—also organized other kinds of parties, at night, at his house a little way up in the mountains. One of the guests must have let something slip out about this, a story that still resonated with lust. But how on earth had this Florines, mixture of serf, hunter, and pimp, become a rebel? *Captain* Florines, no less. Why was he called captain all of a sudden?

I called my clerk. My clerk, who no matter what happened could stay home. Who never, at any time of the day or night, would have to go out to catch or shoot rebels.

You might as well go home at two, I told my clerk. I said this at a quarter past two, when the man had already stayed on at the office of his own accord, because he thought that perhaps he could do something for me. But my own peace of mind depended at that moment on going home at two, and now that damned Florines had turned rebel and I had to go there, my superior had said. Florines a captain. Why?

Why does Florines call himself a captain?, I asked my clerk.

Actually, he was pensioned off, my clerk said.

Impossible, I said. When did he retire?

Ten years ago, my clerk said.

It appeared that Florines had been an officer in one of the three militia corps which, as long as anyone can remember, were made up in this region of volunteers from the mountains.[3] That he was dismissed before he was even forty, on grounds of excessive laziness and incompetence, and that ever since he had been receiving a pension of some sort. Okay. Captain Florines, then.

But suddenly something terrible occurred to me.

Did any soldiers desert?, I asked.

My clerk couldn't say, nor could anyone else for that matter, and then it struck me that I really had very little information and that perhaps I had better wait to see what would happen in the afternoon.

Of course it was absolutely impossible to wait and see what would happen that afternoon. In a few hours my superior was going to call me on the phone. My superior was going to call me when he was through with his bath, his dinner, and his afternoon nap. And what would I say then? I couldn't very well say that I was still waiting for further reports, however true and sensible that might be. And my superior might call sooner, if he in turn were called by his superior when the latter in his turn heard about the burned villages. Those damned villages. If they had not made up those stupid stories, nobody would have heard about this rebellion for days.

Then I thought, again to my horror, that it could actually be true, about those villages. I had rejected the story as nonsensical when it had not yet occurred to me that Captain Florines was that particular Captain Florines. But now that I knew this, matters were quite different. Florines was definitely not your regular Messiah rebel who wrapped himself in a white sheet, gathered disciples around himself, and who finally fought himself to death in some stupid way. Who ever heard of a pimp fighting to death. In a white sheet, no less. On the other hand, such a person might well set fire to villages. And I was suddenly not so sure anymore about my villages.

I went over to the map that hung on the wall of my office. It looked like the two villages which might have been burned down after all were some twenty or thirty miles from my post. Twenty to thirty miles. I glanced at the clock and started counting. I would need half an hour to get a squad of police troops lined up and ready to march. Then it would be three o'clock. Leave at quarter after. Because we would have to go in two separate trucks, and one of them was bound not to start, with the result that after ten minutes of exhaustive moaning and groaning of the starter they would have to crank it by hand. Fine. At a quarter past three we would leave. We would not arrive at the first village until a little before five, but surely that should be early enough.

Because there were two possibilities: either that village had been burned down and if so, there would be enough to do to keep us from thinking about going on to the other village. Or the village had not been burned down and if so, the second village would also be undamaged. In that case we could calmly gather some information on the spot. In the evening I would phone in an extensive report to my chief, and tomorrow we would finish the case. Having gotten this far, I became less and less sorry about my lost afternoon nap.

You can really go home now, I told my clerk.

But I first would like to send for some food for you, my clerk said.

A good man. I nodded as friendly as I could. In a little while twenty-six hefty men would be lining up in front of my office, all of them with carbines slung over their shoulders and revolvers on their hips, oh yes, also sabers. They would click their heels and their commander would report to me. Damn it, I had completely forgotten to notify their commander.

I phoned the commander and explained the case to him. In the meantime, my clerk came in with a man who, rather solemnly, carried my food on a tray. When I was done with the phone calls, I sat down at my desk, using it as a dinner table. Seldom have I dined with such relish.

I heard the trucks drive up in front of the office as I was attentively peeling an apple, and a little later the commander pushed open the door. He was a big heavy man with a fat red face. He stopped in the doorway and reported that his little guys were all present. Really, that's what he said. My little guys are present, he said. Still chewing, I went to get my cap.

Aren't you taking any weapons?, the fat man asked. Of course, where did I keep that bitch, that pistol, in the drawer in my desk, and not loaded, of course. There was a box with cartridges with it. I put the whole lot in my pocket.

Would you like a piece of apple?, I asked the commander.

Well, if I am not depriving you. That's what he said.

All was well, everything was splendid. When I went out, they all clicked their heels. They had kept the engines of their trucks running, smart boys, smart little guys. They had to stand in the trucks, they held on to the sides and to each other. At first I wanted to stand up too, but I noticed that the commander was sitting next to the driver in the other car, and I didn't want to embarrass him. Before a quarter to three we were on the highway already. It might even turn out to be a quickie.

The weather was marvelous, warm, and wherever we passed there were only a few people to be seen. We drove rather fast and I thought that actually we might even have a look at both villages. If the first one hadn't been burned down, that is, something that I began to believe in less and less again. Yeah, that Florines was crazy. He'd go and burn down villages, of course, where a lot of his friends were living.

After a rather sharp curve, the blue mountains lay before us. As soon as we had passed the small forest at the right-hand side of the road, the first village would come in sight.

We were past the forest and I did not see the village. I only heard a few confused exclamations from the men behind me. And then I saw that there was nothing to see anymore. That only a few charred remnants were left standing. The village had been burned. As burned as could be.

Florines had not only burned down this village but also two others, three in all. Fortunately, the third village was not much more than a hamlet close to the second one, so I would not have to take separate notice of it, if need be. It was bad enough as it was.

I decided to hold a council of war. It was high time, too.

We made the vehicles stop somewhere. I had originally planned to drive on to the center of the village, but I couldn't find it anymore, the center. There had been some sort of square before, but now it was all square. Some people were searching through the ruins and a few were sitting on stones. They stared at us. Of course. There wasn't much else to look at.

Half an hour later I had sufficient details from as many as twenty mouths, to get a concrete idea of what had happened. Captain Florines had come to the village yesterday afternoon with fifty strangers. He had gone to the village square and because his arrival was an unusual occurrence, the villagers had followed him, to see what would happen. Most inhabitants of the village had already returned from working the land, and it must have been pretty crowded in that little square with Florines waiting at the head of those strange men, so to speak, until everyone was present to hear what he had to say. They hadn't worn any white clothes, Florines and his men, but they had carried guns. And cartridge belts, at least three per man. That could turn into something yet. Well. Florines had told them that they all had to leave the village. He became like a wild man when they didn't leave immediately, when they—quite understandably, by the way— remained standing in the square, looking at Florines with quizzical expressions and without saying anything.

And suddenly a large flame had leapt up from one of the houses behind Florines's back. I imagined the way Florines had stood there in front of all those people, and had said: Get out! Get out, all of you! And how those people had kept on staring at him, not saying anything, all those questioning eyes. And how Florines had gone wild and had set a house on fire. God knows why he had wanted to empty the village. Maybe he had only wanted to see an empty village in front of him. In a strange way, it is wonderful to see a place empty that usually is teeming with people. I once passed through a small town in Auvergne in the month of October. A so-called spa during the summer months and in December it was winter sports. But in October and November it lay stiffened in the grip of absolute desolation. The place was quite fashionably fitted out. The street signs could be illuminated at night. The sidewalks were wide and expensively paved, and it was all hotels next to fancy shops and shops next to fancy hotels. But everywhere the metal blinds were down. And not a soul was to be heard. At the time it gave me a sense of pride, almost a sense of power. It seemed as if I had been the only one who had had enough strength to survive in this world. I remember how, at an intersection, I got on top of an almost six-feet-high stand for directing traffic, very fancily put together, to take a leak, and hear it splash on the asphalt and hear it echo between the houses. Maybe Florines had wanted something like that too.

If so, he had gotten what he wanted. The fire in the first house had spread immediately to the adjoining one, and the people, moving with even more speed than the fire, had disappeared from the square and from the village, and Florines must have been able to look for a while at a complete desolation before the crackling of the flames had overcome everything else and the heat of the flames had forced him to retreat, too.

This had taken place yesterday afternoon and night. Yesterday afternoon and night Florines had moved out of this burning village in order to set fire to two more villages and then to vanish and camp for the night in the mountains. And I had simply slept that night in my bed and fooled around in my office the next morning. I had told my superior that it was ludicrous to speak of burned villages, and here I stood among the charred debris, while Florines looked down on me from yonder hazy heights. For that matter, Florines may have simply returned to his own house. In fact, that would be most likely, and therefore most humiliating to me. Florines, who, after going on his arson rampage, had calmly returned home with his fifty men. He had kept the fifty men with him, of course. But Lord above, twenty-four hours had already passed since then. The men from the burned village stood around us. They stood watching us, their help, which had come twenty-four hours too late. Actually, they weren't really looking, they just stood and stared. And I had to go back. It was four thirty, and I should go back. If need be, I could drive on to the other village, but no matter what, I would have to file a report this very night. A report about two burned villages and a rebel who, after what he had perpetrated, had calmly gone to sleep in his own house.

I summoned the commander. We're going to the other village, I said curtly.

We drove to the other village. It was the logical thing to do. I climbed on the same truck as the commander and we drove along through country that was dead silent. Dead silent, until the commander nudged me. He pointed across from him. I looked in that direction, but I didn't see anything.

I don't see anything, I said.

There, by those bushes, shouted the commander impatiently.

I heard the men standing on the truck talk excitedly, but I still didn't see anything. I looked at the commander and motioned to slow down. The commander bent over the driver, and we drove more slowly. We stopped, even. I pretended now that I had seen something too. The policemen jumped off the truck and so did the commander, but I kept looking. Then I finally saw something. A group of figures emerged from the bushes and moved in our direction.

There they come!, I yelled. As if anybody hadn't noticed already. There came Captain Florines at the head of his men. Captain Florines was going to engage in battle with his pursuers. At that moment I thought of the wild boar for the first time, of the wounded boar that emerges from a forest, to charge at his pursuers.

All of a sudden I realized that the cartridges for my pistol were still in my pocket. I was going to encounter the enemy with an unloaded pistol, for it wouldn't do, of course, to get the little box of cartridges out of my pocket at this tense moment. I would have to break open a carefully packed and sealed box of cartridges and then I would have to load my pistol. Such evidence of not being prepared would rob me of the troop's confidence at one blow. I decided simply to pull out my pistol, and if they started shooting, they probably wouldn't notice that I was not shooting along with them.

Those must be fellows from the second village, I heard the commander say.

I quickly put the pistol away. Of course they were men from the second village that Florines had burned. They came from that same direction, but had cut straight across the countryside.

They were indeed from the second village, and the story they told deviated a little from that of the inhabitants of the first village. Florines and his men had not first summoned everybody but had started immediately to pillage a couple of houses and then set fire to them. Moreover, they had kicked and beaten the people, and finally all the villagers had fled. And then the village had gone up in flames behind them. After that, Florines had moved eastward with his gang and had likewise pillaged and burned a village located there. After that, nothing else was heard about him. They thought he was up in the mountains. At any rate, he had not come this way.

I asked one of the fugitives if the village had been completely burned down.

Yes, completely. Nothing was left standing.

In that case, I said to the commander, it makes little sense to go to that village.

The commander expressed doubt about this. Perhaps we will find some traces there, he said.

I looked at him and saw that he was serious. Find traces? Whose? The arsonist's? The only thing I wanted to know was where Florines was, and surely a village burned down twenty-four hours earlier was not the place to look for an answer to that. But perhaps the commander was right. Perhaps the old and tried method used by the police would also be best in this case. To keep on going after a criminal until you got him. But first I wanted to try one more time.

Shouldn't we go to Florines's house first?, I asked.

The commander firmly nodded no. We better go to the other village first, sir, he said.

I began to believe that the man was right. Of course the man was right, even if I didn't know why. And it was also very good for my position if we continued to the second village. I could write a more extensive report then. I would come home later, and the later I came home, the later it would be when I had to relate my unpleasant message by phone.

At that very moment I got an excellent idea.

You're right, I said to the commander. It really is the best thing to do if we follow the trail. It may be old, the trail, but it's still better to keep following it. However, we must take care not to let it get older.

How do you mean?, asked the commander. First we have to go to the second village, I said, and then we'll also have to go to the hamlet, of course, and then we'll set up camp in the area. 'Cause, if we go home first and start all over again tomorrow, we would lose too much time.

There's something to that, the commander said.

I blushed with pleasure. It's human nature, but I blushed with pleasure.

Furthermore, I said eagerly, if we stay out here, Florines will think twice before burning down any more villages.

Possibly, the commander said, possibly.

We decided to send one truck and four men back to get the equipment necessary for our camp. Mostly blankets and coffee. In addition, I asked for a towel, a bar of soap, and a toothbrush for myself. We didn't need reinforcements, the commander felt. That was fine with me. I would not have to make a report tonight. I couldn't be reached by phone even. I gave the officers a note for my clerk. He was to let my superior know that I was hunting down Florines and that I would not come back before I had him. That would make an enormous impression. I was very pleased with myself.

The men got in the remaining truck, and the other one went back. We continued southward. We came closer and closer to the foot of the blue mountains. After twenty minutes we came to a second village. It was definitely, completely burned down. We found a group of about thirty people, men, women, and children. I asked where the others were.

Well, the others had gone looking for shelter with friends and relatives. Why haven't you?, I asked.

Well, they didn't come from this area and they didn't know anybody here.

We will have to send these people over to the district capital, I said to the commander. They can't stay out here in the open for another night.

They can stay at the police barracks, said the commander. There's enough room there now. So we also sent the other truck down with the thirty rather bewildered people in it, while we headed south on foot, past the burned hamlet, to where there was supposed to be a large farm. There we would set up camp, that is to say, if Florines hadn't burned that down too.

Couldn't Florines himself be there?, I asked the commander. Certainly not, said the commander, Florines has gone further, and I think I know where he is. I have sent for a map from the barracks and then we will figure it out precisely.

That was fine with me. I wanted to look for Florines and I wanted to find him, but I had no desire to see him tonight. I was fed up with Florines, it was as if he had stayed with me for a three-day visit.

The farm was still standing and Florines wasn't there. He had been there, all right, late last night, but he had continued on his way.

He and his men had butchered a cow and even paid for it. They had taken the meat with them and had continued south. I thought it was quite reassuring.

A fire was made, dinner was cooked, and an hour later the commander and I were seated with large steaming plates in front of us. In the meantime the trucks had returned and the commander had his map. After dinner we spread it out on the table, put an oil lamp on it, and started a game of strategy by the yellow light.

According to the map, there was a mountain pass that started close to our farm. It ran south through the mountains and eventually descended to sea level on the other side. According to the commander, Florines would have crossed this pass and continued along the coast until he had presumably arrived at a fishing village about twenty miles to the east. Once there, he would have stolen or rented a ship to flee to safety.

I did not believe it. I could not picture Florines on a ship. Moreover, if it were true, we might just as well go home right away, for then we would never catch up with him.

Where is Florines's house, exactly?, I asked.

The commander pointed out a spot to me, roughly fifty miles in a southwesterly direction. But he can't get there from here, he said. He would have to pass the mountains on this side and then we would certainly have run into him.

We finally decided that the next day we would go through the pass until we reached the coast. If we didn't find any traces of Florines there, we would head westward into the mountains, if need be, all the way to Florines's house, and then go back to our base. It looked like it was going to be a two-day trip.

When we got up from our deliberations we heard somebody shout, and a little later we heard two shots, one after the other. The first thing I thought was, dammit, I still forgot to load my pistol. And then: Florines has come back. Florines did not go on any ship. He won't have us walk to the coast for nothing. I got the feeling that it was nice of Florines not to let us down. Something like what a hunter must feel when, not having shot anything all day, he unexpectedly finds some game staring right down the barrel of his gun.

One of the policemen had fired the shot. He had seen someone sneak around the farm. He had called out to him, and when there was no reply he had fired a shot.

And that second shot?, asked the commander.

Well, the policeman had shot twice.

I'll send a couple of guys down there right away, said the commander. He didn't go himself, so I didn't think it was necessary for me to go either. I unfolded the map once more. West of the pass that we would take tomorrow was a mountain top. 3,543 feet, it said. I had the feeling Florines would be there.

I summoned the owner of the farm. I pointed out the mountain top to him.

Does someone live there?, I asked.

There was a house on the mountain top. There was a house where hunters spend the night sometimes.

Florines is there, I thought. He's there tonight and he'll be there again tomorrow night.

I went to the room where I was going to sleep. I took the pistol from my pocket and the box of cartridges. Outside in the yard I heard the commander's voice.

Did they find anything?, I yelled.

No, they hadn't found anything. I went back to my pistol and loaded it. I put it under my pillow. Tomorrow the hunt would begin. The first hunt I was to be part of as an armed man. The hunt for a quarry that would surely be kind enough not to go outside our territory.

Actually, it was going to be my second hunt in twenty years. Twenty years ago was my first hunt, and that first hunt had left me with a feeling of kinship with the hunted quarry.

As a boy of eighteen I once joined the beaters for a hunt. At the time I lived in the Veluwe, in the Netherlands, south of the Royal Domain, and I was in love with a girl on the north side. Prince Henry, the Queen's consort, had been dead for two years already, and the boars he could no longer hunt were abundant. Very abundant. They streamed from the area reserved for them into the surrounding forests and acreage. They even came into the gardens of the villages and uprooted the flower beds. I could hear them grunt at night when I crossed the crown land on my bicycle from north to south, which was strictly forbidden. They belonged with the forest, the way the creaking of the trees belonged with the forest. There was nothing frightening about those boars. To encounter a gamekeeper would have been a lot worse. A gamekeeper yelled: Stop!, get off your bike!, and then he'd put his own bicycle across the road in a very irritating way, and you had to get off and he produced a dog-eared pad from the breast pocket of his coat, and then he licked his pencil stub and wrote, all the time stinking of corduroy. A wild boar didn't do any of this. A wild boar just grunted in the undergrowth and remained invisible, almost as if apologizing.

Only on rare occasions did I get to see a wild boar. One of those occasions did indeed make a profound impression on me. I was just outside the crown land, near one of the swing-gates that could be pulled open by means of a wire strap. I had left the Domain through this gate when I saw a wild boar coming toward me at a distance of about a hundred yards. It ran down the road in my direction. In the distance I heard confused shouting and I understood that the animal was being hunted. When the boar saw me, it swerved from the direction it was running in. It took me for a new danger it had to dodge, but in the meantime it had gotten so close that I could hear it pant from exertion. And the way it was running, it suddenly looked like my own fat little dog, and maybe that's why I felt sorry for it. I swung the gate open by the strap and stepped aside. The animal saw its escape and rushed past me, panting all the time, and I immediately closed the gate behind him. Then I bicycled away and a little later wound up in the middle of a group of pursuers who had lost track. They said nothing and I said nothing. The Veluwe people rarely get excited.

I myself escaped from a gamekeeper once. I saw the man calmly pedaling toward me at about a hundred yards distance, and I was pedaling his way. A snake and a little songbird. A snake on a bike, and a little songbird on a bike. Suddenly I felt such furious pity for myself that I jumped off my bike and rushed into the underbrush with it. I threw the bicycle in a pit because it was hampering my flight. I ran on until I came to a dirt wall of what in the Domain was called the Second Java Fort. There were two forts called Java Fort. They had been built by King William the Third, around 1870. The

King in those days—in fact, during his entire life—was particularly embittered against the Prussians, and expected them to attack in the course of time. This King lived out his daydreams—he must have had both beautiful and horrifying ones—by building these two forts. The first Java Fort had turned out to be a star-shaped earthen citadel. Because it had been opened to the public it was completely worn down. Children shouted and slid down the walls in the dry shallow moat, while inside, those who were a little older attempted some hectic lovemaking that was constantly interrupted.

But the second fort was in a strictly forbidden area and was probably still in the same state as when it was built by the King. The wall was rectangular and at least nine feet high, and so densely overgrown that it had turned into the fortress of a sleeping beauty. If you didn't know it existed, you could walk past it within a few yards without seeing anything else than an amazingly dense and tangled column of scrub pine.

I ran toward this fortress. I knew there was an entrance at each of the four corners. When I had entered the inner court, which was also filled with trees and bushes, I dropped to the ground, gasping for breath. I panted heavily but cautiously. I didn't want to betray my presence. I panted the way the wild boar had panted. At that moment I felt like a boar threatened by hunters and, grunting all the time, I felt very sorry for myself.

I must have stayed like that for an hour, when the metamorphosis from fear, the pity, and the romanticism gave way to boredom. I got up and left the fortress. I went back in the direction of King's Lane. My bicycle was still in the pit and the gamekeeper was nowhere to be found. It was possible that the man had not seen me at all.

In the end, the wild boars caused so much annoyance to the farmers in the surrounding area that various drives were organized. I participated in one of these hunts as a beater. It was the most inconsistent thing I could have done, after my encounter with the fat panting animal and my own metamorphosis in the Second Java Fort, but I did it anyway. The wild boar was going to be driven from an oak forest near the home of the girl I was in love with, and the girl herself was going to join in the hunt.

There were twenty beaters in all, and two men with guns were in the firebreak toward which the boars were supposed to be driven. We beaters took up our position. We had all brought big sticks to beat against the trees, and we yelled: Koy, koy, and made a tremendous racket.

When we had gone through about three quarters of the terrain and there still hadn't been a shot, we calmed down a little. The enthusiasm had gone. We slowly began to realize that the boar could very well be in another forest.

Suddenly I heard the girl yell. I immediately ran in her direction. I would even have gone for the boar with my stick. But as I got closer, I heard that she was not calling for me but for Albert. Albert was her father's tenant farmer, and at this important moment in her life she apparently put more trust in him than she did in me. And it was Albert who showed up a little ahead of me, but there wasn't any boar to be seen. Maybe the animal had escaped in the spot I had just left. Maybe it was the same boar I had helped escape a few days earlier. Or maybe it was the boar I had been myself, when I had lain panting and grunting in the Second Java Fort. I would have saved it again, but there was no shooting that afternoon, at least at boars. Dejected that when she had been in need, the girl had not called out for me but for Albert, I jumped across the ditch into the firebreak. A shot went off. One of the hunters had taken me for a hunted wild animal. That is how my first hunt ended.

And tomorrow my second hunt would begin. My loaded pistol, my hunting rifle, was under my pillow.

When I woke up the next morning I was oblivious of time, as is usual when you're in unfamiliar surroundings. I got up, dressed, and stepped outside. None of the policemen was in sight. The view in back of the farm was blocked by a row of trees with low branches. I heard water splashing nearby and headed for the sound, passing under the trees until I came into the open. The blue mountains were right in front of me now, and the water was that of a little mountain brook, which spilled over a protruding rock and formed a miniature waterfall.

I took my clothes off and squatted down in the splashing stream of water. I gasped for breath from the piercing cold. The blue mountains were close. Everywhere were rocks like the one I was squatting in front of. Florines could be behind any one of the rocks. I would make the easiest prey for him he could ever wish. But Florines wouldn't shoot. Hunting season was still closed to the two of us for a short while, perhaps for a single hour. For those few moments while I sat there, squatting in the animal comfort of the biting cold water, I was the quarry, the boar, but Florines would not hunt.

I became human again when I discovered that I hadn't brought a towel. Of course, I had left it in my bedroom. I dried myself with my undershirt, dressed, and walked back to the house. A minute later I met the commander. I asked him what he thought about setting a time for departure, and he said that it depended on the route we would take. I thought we had determined that the night before, I said, but the commander was not so sure, after all. So once more we unrolled the map, and then it appeared that the commander had partially sacrificed his night's rest to manufacture a number of pins with little red flags and white flags. He had apparently gotten so much satisfaction out of his otherwise excellently played role as chief of staff that he didn't mind giving a second performance. The little flags were stuck into the map. The red ones were for Florines, the white ones for us.

Those shots got me thinking, the commander said.

Those shots had been the shots of his own policemen, but all right, I was in favor of any change that might bring us closer to the 3,543-foot-high mountain. We decided to follow the mountain pass for the time being, and then hold another council halfway up.

We set out. The trucks were left behind at the farm, under guard of two officers and both drivers.

The road we walked on was hard at first, but it gradually turned into an overgrown trail. When we left, our formation, according to the commander's orders, was that everyone had to follow one another at approximately six feet distance. The commander went first, I came second, and we walked in a long file along the slowly rising path. The blue mountains were before us, the hunting ground stretched solidly and confidently before the hunters. No one spoke. All of us went on with intense concentration.

The hunt had begun.

The speed at which we walked was not fast but very steady. In fact, I saw nothing but the regular motions of the legs of the man in front of me and I moved mine with equal regularity. When I finally glanced back, I saw the plain already receding behind and below us. But at that same moment I lost the rhythm, and it took a while before I was back in step again.

It got hotter. It became tremendously hot. While I kept on walking, I took my shirt off and slung it across my shoulder. I was no longer thinking about Florines. There was nothing left but the monotonous, all-engrossing displacement of legs.

The path became more stony. Loose stones that made walking harder, because they broke the cadence. Finally the commander stopped. He turned around, and I saw his face for the first time since the beginning of the trip. It had turned fire red. The policemen stood around us. I believe I was too tired and too stiff to sit down. I leaned against the wall of the pass.

The commander stated that we were about halfway, that we would rest for an hour and then decide in which direction to go. In the meantime I had found a few shady bushes and dropped to the ground beneath them. The others looked for a similar place. Nobody said anything. Everyone was dead tired.

We had been lying like that for perhaps half an hour, when I heard voices. I sat up and saw the policeman look and point in the direction we had just come from. I asked what was going on. It turned out to be the two officers we had left with the trucks. They climbed the pass rather quickly. When they had reached us, they came straight up to me. They even clicked their heels, and one of the two handed me a letter. It was a letter from my clerk.

Dear sir. This morning at 7:00 A.M. thirty-four persons belonging to Captain Florines's gang reported to the police barracks. Their weapons were taken away and they have been taken into protective custody. Captain Florines has not been caught yet. Yours truly.

I handed the letter to the commander. What do you think of this?, I asked.

Well, said the commander, well, that changes matters, of course. Those men must have started fighting, or they got scared.

Would Florines have gone back to his own house?, I asked.

Possibly, said the commander, possibly.

He wouldn't have fled by sea, I said.

Probably not, said the commander. We will find out when we interrogate the prisoners.

So you want to go back first?, I asked.

It is the best thing to do, said the commander. Otherwise, it will be like looking for a needle in a haystack.

Of course he was right. We had to go back. The descent would be easy and rather quick. We would find the trucks near the farmhouse, and we would be home before dark. The hunt had failed.

Give me five men, I suddenly told the commander. I'm going to take a look by that mountain. If Florines isn't there, I'll come back down from there.

We got the map to check it out. It was a possibility, the commander thought. He could send the trucks back to a certain point along the road down below, and that way I would also be home that same night.

Half an hour later I was alone with my five men, my hunting companions. The commander had given me his map, and we had taken everything that was drinkable from the others. When they were gone, we calmly sat down for another quarter of an hour. I studied the map once more with the oldest of the remaining policemen, and we agreed on what road to follow.

Now it became a real climb. The oldest man led the way and we followed. After we had climbed around and over rocks for a while, the ground became less rocky, and eventually we came to a forest. There we rested again. The forest was dense and it was rather cool. Good hunters that we were, we had slowly gotten a feeling of certainty that we were on the track of the game, although we could not back it up with anything logical.

As soon as we are out of these woods, the oldest officer said, we'll have to climb for another hour and then we will be on top. We'd better climb it on this side. On this side there are only a few rocks.

Away from the forest the ground was indeed free of stones. We climbed on without resting. The surroundings were ideal for approaching the game in its shelter. Close to the summit were bushes and low trees to provide cover.

Finally we reached the top. We squatted in the bushes and looked at the house standing in the middle of the flattened mountain top. It seemed completely abandoned. A shutter in front of one of the windows rattled and creaked in the wind.

We left the bushes. After all, we had to search the house. We stole up on it carefully.

Then, like a hunter who suddenly sees a better and more advantageous spot than his fellow hunters, I took a left turn around the house, while the others turned right.

I went left around the house. I tiptoed past a hedge that grew around the backyard. I had my pistol in my hand.

I heard something. I heard the sound of falling water. I peeked through the hedge.

A man was standing by a round stone well. He held a little bucket in his hand which he used to scoop up water and then pour it over his head. He had his back turned to me, but I recognized Florines.

It was Florines, but he was now also the wild boar and I was no longer the hunter. A boar at its watering hole and I had to warn it. I had to chase it into the safe underbrush before the others caught it. I had to save my friend the boar.

Psst, I called, psssst.

The boar didn't hear, it must have been deafened by the water in its ears.

Hey! I yelled, hey! Then the boar turned around.

I saw Florines's face. Florines's pale, somewhat puffy face, Florines's mean and dirty face, with water dripping from it. He looked straight into the setting sun, and perhaps that was why it seemed as if he were grinning. I had stuck my hands through the hedge, the pistol in my right hand. I fired a shot. Florines flung his arms up in the air and took a tremendous leap. He landed on his legs and, as if set off by a spring, he leaped again, and once more, his arms always up in the air. Then he crashed forward to the ground. Flat.

I was still standing by the hedge when the policemen were bending over Florines.

He is dead!, they yelled. Dead as a doornail! Right through his head.

I stood by the hedge. I felt something on my right hand. I looked at it. It was my index finger, my bent index finger, which had been around the trigger. I stretched it with my left hand, but a little later I felt it again, my bent index finger.

One of the policemen asked if they should carry Florines down the mountain.

For God's sake no, I said. For God's sake no.

I went over to it. They had rolled him over.

Put him back the way he was, I said. I could, if need be, believe again that this wasn't Florines, if he were lying face down. We won't take him along, I said. We will burn him here. He burned villages, now we will also burn him.

This vengeance completely satisfied my policemen. They started collecting wood right away, and soon an enormous pyre had been erected.

Put him on it, face down, I said.

They did. Light the wood, I said. A little later the flames leaped up on all sides. They laughed, the policemen, they thought it was a splendid joke on my part to still be able to fool Florines like this. But actually I was not even thinking about Florines any more. I saw only the flames, my last salute to the boar, my friend.

When the flames threatened to die out, the policemen again threw wood on it. It had become dark now, and the flames illuminated the house and our faces. The wood crackled, and the policemen shouted and laughed.

But at last everything grew quiet. The fire died down and it was dark. Dark and terribly cold. It had become bitterly, so bitterly cold after the burning of Captain Florines.

The Treasure

RUNNING from west to east along nearly the entire length of our main island, there was a hundred-mile range of mountains and hills which we called the divide, because rainwater streamed down its slopes in little brooks either to the north or to the south. The water ran down without being obstructed, the stones did not hold anything back, and there were no tree roots because there were no trees, said the forester, and he thought some things were a disgrace. He said: In the drawer of my desk I have a complete plan for the reforestation of the divide.

The harbor master said he had just thrown three jacks, and that he was going to let them stand, and that they weren't sitting at their office desks at the moment. The harbor master put the dice back into the cup and, bowing politely, passed it on to his neighbor, Mr. Zeinal. Everyone was always polite to Mr. Zeinal. Mr. Zeinal shook the cup and threw.

Too bad, that's not enough, Mr. Zeinal, said the harbor master.

I rather think that I didn't get anything at all, said Mr. Zeinal.

Come on, doctor, you old bastard!, shouted the harbor master.

Come on, doctor, you old bastard!, we all shouted. The doctor shook the cup.

It is a good thing that you have a plan for the divide, Mr. Zeinal told the forester. Something certainly should be done about it. But it will be difficult.

My boss had told me that Mr. Zeinal was opposed to the forester's plans for reforestation. He has something against it, my boss had said. And you can bet your life that you won't get a single tree planted on the divide if Mr. Zeinal won't have it.

Problems can be solved, the forester said.

Four aces, the doctor said.

Trees slurp up all the water, said Taronggi III. Taronggi III was known as a submissive friend of Mr. Zeinal.

We ought to do something about that divide, the harbor master said.

There's money to be made with the divide, the surveyor said.

Four aces, the doctor said once more.

There are treasures in the divide, the surveyor said.

How so, treasures?, the forester asked.

Treasures just for the taking, said the surveyor.

That quieted us all down.

What kind of treasures, Taronggi III finally asked. Rubies? Deep down somewhere in one of the rooms of his dark house, Taronggi III kept a small statue under a bell jar, and the statue was literally covered with rubies from top to bottom.[1] My boss had held it in his hands, Taronggi III had not dared refuse him, and my boss had counted the rubies. Two hundred rubies he had counted, and each one of them was firmly attached.

Gold?, Mr. Zeinal asked.

My servant knew that Mr. Zeinal had fifty bags of gold hidden under his house. One bag for every year of his life, my servant had said, and every bag too heavy for one man to pick up.

Nicols, the surveyor said,

I see, the habor master said.

What are nicols?, Taronggi III asked.

Feldspar, the surveyor said.[2]

What is Feldspar, precisely?, Mr. Zeinal asked.

Feldspar, Mr. Zeinal?, the harbor master said. Feldspar is a mineral.

They make nicol prisms out of it, Mr. Zeinal, said the surveyor.[3]

Nicol prisms are used in all kinds of instruments, the forester said.

Prism-binoculars, for example, the harbor master said.

And you can make money from that?, Taronggi III asked.

If there is enough to make exploitation profitable, said the forester.

There's enough, said the surveyor. There's enough to make us all rich.

To make us all rich, we all said. The surveyor is going to make all of us rich.

We have to establish a company, said the harbor master.

A joint-stock company, said the forester.

Apply for a concession, said the harbor master.

The doctor emptied his glass of rum. He said: We ought to go there.

Of course we should go there. And we went. We rushed out of the club to our cars. We had four cars and there were seven of us. The harbor master didn't want to drive. He asked: Can I come with you, Mr. Zeinal?

You're coming with me, said Mr. Zeinal, Mr. Taronggi too, and who else of the gentlemen?

I was one of those gentlemen. I sat next to Mr. Zeinal's driver and the three others crowded together in the back. The doctor and the surveyor led the way in the doctor's car, and the forester went by himself in his own car. Nobody wanted to ride with the forester. Nobody wanted to listen to his plan for reforestation. We wanted to go to the treasure.

Do you think there is something to it?, I heard Taronggi III ask in the back. I didn't know who he was asking, but Mr. Zeinal replied. There are many old tales about treasures, said Mr. Zeinal. There is a story about one of the kings who married a young woman who knew the art of changing all sorts of things into gold. She also communicated often with mountain spirits, and one day she met a spirit who sat crying on top of his mountain. She asked him why he was crying, and the spirit said that his mountain was in the shadow of a taller mountain, which robbed him of sunlight. The golden sunlight never shines upon my mountain, complained the spirit. Well, that was no problem for the king's wife, and she changed the top of the crying spirit's mountain into pure gold. But when the king heard what she had done, he got terribly angry.

That's understandable, said the harbor master.

The king thought that his wife had cheated on him, said Mr. Zeinal. He went out to look for the spirit and when he couldn't find him, he smashed the mountain top into a thousand pieces, which flew in all directions. One of the pieces is still supposed to be in the ground next to the house of our prince.

But it isn't gold the surveyor has found, is it?, Taronggi III asked.

Nicols, said the harbor master.

When I looked back a little later to contribute to the conversation, all three of them were asleep on the back seat.

The doctor preceded us and the forester followed us. I saw the doctor slow down and signal with his hand. He turned into a narrow side road. We followed him and the forester followed us. The side road became increasingly bumpy, narrow, and overgrown. We also were climbing, we were coming into the mountains. A few times we almost broke the shock absorbers of the car, and the three in the back woke up.

Lousy road, the harbor master said. We better walk.

Perhaps it isn't too far anymore, Mr. Zeinal said.

That's why, the harbor master said.

We had been driving down the side road for about ten minutes when the doctor stopped. We stopped behind him and a little later the forester pulled up.

Are we walking the rest of the way?, the harbor master asked.

Yes, the surveyor said, there's no road anymore.

You call this a road?, the forester asked.

There's a small country cottage nearby that belongs to the prince, Mr. Zeinal said.

Does someone live there?, Taronggi III asked.

Maybe we can get something to eat there, the harbor master said. I'm hungry.

We were all hungry. We climbed the path. The surveyor, Mr. Zeinal, and Taronggi III went first, followed by the doctor and the harbor master. The doctor carried two bottles of Dutch gin and a bottle of rum. Soon we came to the cottage of the prince. There were people in it. One of the prince's servants lived there with his wife and a couple of children. We sat on the porch of the house and Mr. Zeinal said that we wanted to eat, and the prince's servant went to the back of the house. The doctor called him back again. He handed him the bottles and asked him to open them. After a moment, the servant's son returned with the open bottles and a tinkling tray of glasses. We also heard a tremendous cackling in back of the house.

They're killing a chicken, said the forester.

They should have killed a goat, said the harbor master. I am hungry.

Mr. Zeinal called the servant again. He asked if it was possible to kill a goat. The servant said it was possible, but that already five chickens had been killed.

Oh, that's fine too, said the harbor master.

Should they kill a goat anyway?, Mr. Zeinal asked.

No, certainly not, Mr. Zeinal, said the harbor master. Five chickens will be fine. Five chickens, that's more than enough.

How come you always drink nothing else but rum, doctor, asked the forester.

Because I like rum, the doctor said.

Too syrupy for me, said the forester.

Good rum is not syrupy, said the harbor master.

We drank and sat quietly. We sat quietly looking at the mountains around us. The sun went down.

That tall peak there is made of gold, Taronggi III said.

You'd like that, wouldn't you, said the forester.

That happened long ago, said Taronggi III.

A story Mr. Zeinal told us, said the harbor master.

There ought to be trees on those mountains, said the forester.

The servant and his son brought each a big tray with roasted meat. They put the trays down on the table between our glasses and we ate the meat while we kept on drinking, except for Mr. Zeinal and Taronggi III. Outside the shadows became longer and longer. It was dead silent and we no longer talked. We ate and we drank.

It's really beautiful here, the harbor master finally said.

It's growing dark, said the forester. We must head home.

We still have to pay, said the harbor master.

Please, let me take care of it, said Mr. Zeinal.

No, certainly not, Mr. Zeinal, said the harbor master.

Please, I insist, said Mr. Zeinal.

Then we will share the bill, Mr. Zeinal, said the harbor master.

Gladly, said Mr. Zeinal.

The surveyor has fallen asleep, said the forester.

We shook the surveyor's chair and yelled: Wake up!

Huh, said the surveyor.

We're going home, we said.

I want to go to the treasure, said the surveyor.

Treasure?, we asked.

He means the nicols, said the forester.

Tomorrow, the harbor master promised. Tomorrow. It's too dark now.

Fine, said the surveyor, very good. Tomorrow.

Are the gentlemen all leaving?, the doctor asked. I said I didn't mind staying for a while.

The doctor and I stood on the porch to wave goodbye to the others. A little later we heard the engines start and we heard them drive off. We sat down again. The doctor filled the glasses. There was one small piece of meat left on one of the dishes.

You take it, the doctor said.

You take it, I said.

No, you, said the doctor.

I took it.

The Last Island

OLON and I were sitting on top of the small cabin of the Hecuba, and we could hear Mrs. Olon swear from the deck of the Arimassa.[1] It had been a strange affair with the Arimassa at the time. They had built her on the largest of the northern islands, and when she was to be launched, they had asked us to cable her name. That telegram was brought to us when we were sitting in the club, and we were already three rounds behind because of the dice game, and we thought it a good joke to give the ship the name Threemaster. For two reasons: first, the ship did not have any masts at all, it was to become a small tugboat and second, because of the complications when the Threemaster would have to give her name at sea.

What's the name of your ship?

Threemaster.

What's the name of your threemaster?

Threemaster.

What's the name of your threemaster, damn it?

We thought this could make for very amusing conversations, and so we telegraphed to the northern island: Name ship colon threemaster.

I have always regarded it as the most normal thing in the world that the telegram arrived garbled. At any rate, Threemaster was not called Threemaster but Arimassa. A baptism is a baptism, a name is a name.

Olon and his wife had been to my office the day before, looking for swimmers. There had to be swimmers living on one of our islands, Olon had said. Swimmers who could do everything. Olon needed the best swimmers available. They have to fish for me, Olon said. They have to swim after the nets for me. I have to have the best swimmers.

I asked: On which island are these swimmers supposed to live?

Olon flung his wallet on the table. Money was bulging out on all sides.

I'll pay, said Olon.

Yes, I said, all right. But what's the name of the island?

We will find it, Olon said. We will sail there. We will sail all over. We will ask. Here and there and everywhere. And we will hear stories about swimmers. About swimmers who can do everything. And then we'll know that we are there.

Olon had his schooner, the Hecuba, in our harbor. We were going to take the Hecuba to look for the island of the swimmers. Olon, Mrs. Olon, and I, even if it would take a month.

Enough provisions on board, Olon said. Enough beer and rum.

When I heard about the rum, I asked if the doctor could come too. To examine the swimmers, I was going to say, but Olon already said that it was all right. But the doctor did not want to come with us. Give him a bottle of rum anyway, I said.

He can go to hell, Olon said.

We left the same evening. We had eaten beforehand on shore, and on board we drank. It was very calm. Dead calm.

It will be windy once we get further from shore, Olon said.

He pushed the Hecuba away from the shore with a hook and hoisted the main sail. It did not stir.

Whistle for wind!, Olon yelled to his wife.

Mrs. Olon whistled, but there came no wind.

Whistle!, Olon yelled.

Mrs. Olon whistled, I whistled, but nothing happened. We turned in a circle, very slowly, ten feet from shore.

Olon yelled, Mrs. Olon whistled, and I went down to the cabin. There was a mattress on the floor. I lay down on it and slept.

I woke to a loud thud. When I went up, I saw that we were moored again.

There's no wind, Olon said. We won't set sail tonight. We'll sail tomorrow morning. There's always wind in the morning.

The next morning there was wind, but not enough to please Olon.

We'll take a tugboat, Olon said. Do you have a tugboat here?

I told him of the Arimassa, and so at half past ten in the morning we left, we, Olon and I, on the Hecuba, pulled by the Arimassa. We had put Mrs. Olon on the Arimassa. We saw her standing next to the deckhouse and heard her swear at the crew. I had brought a map of our islands with me, and I showed it to Olon.

Where are we going?, I asked.

To the island of the swimmers, Olon said.

Which island?, I asked.

We'll find it, Olon said.

I yelled to the captain of the Arimassa, to ask where we were going. He yelled back a name.

This is where we are going, I said, and I pointed out the island to Olon, the name of which the captain had yelled to me. An eight-hour sail.

Are there swimmers there?, Olon asked.

I don't know, I said.

We'll find them, Olon said.

In the evening we sailed into the small harbor of the island. It was very quiet there.

No one lives here, Olon said.

Oh yes, I said, but it's dark. The people have gone home. They want to sleep.

We have to call them together, Olon said. We have to hear stories. Stories about swimmers.

I had them bring us to the house of the chief of the island. The chief was working in a small office next to his house, by the light of an oil lamp. He was filling in the tax lists, he said.

We have to gather the people together, Olon said.

The chief said that it was too late. The next morning he would have the people together.

Are there swimmers on this island?, Olon asked.

The chief said that there were fishermen.

Can they also swim?, Olon asked.

No, swim they didn't.

We have to talk to the fishermen tomorrow, Olon said. We have to hear stories about swimmers.

The next morning the chief had all the men of the island gather together.

Are the fishermen here?, Olon asked.

Yes, the fishermen were in the front rows.

Have them tell stories, Olon said.

But no one said anything, except the chief. The chief told us how the men often went on long journeys, sometimes lasting for weeks, and that they saw a lot of the world. But there were no stories about swimmers. No, they had never heard of an island where men were famous for their swimming. Yes, it was possible that such an island existed, but in any case they wouldn't know where it could be.

We stayed on the island for the rest of the day, and the next morning we sailed on. We let ourselves be towed again by the Arimassa. Only Olon went on board the tugboat with his wife. I was lying on top of the cabin of the Hecuba. I heard the water splash against the bow. I heard the sea rustling past the sides. I ate, I drank, I slept.

The evening of that day we arrived too late at the island to go ashore. One of the sailors of the Arimassa got a mattress for Mrs. Olon, who stayed on board there. Olon came to the Hecuba.

The next morning we went ashore, and in an hour the men were gathered together. Yes, they were mostly fishermen. No, they did not swim. No, they did not know any stories about swimmers.

The next morning we were on the next island. And there was an old man at the meeting, in the front row. He said that he had once heard of an island where there were very good swimmers.

Which island?, Olon asked.

Well, he did not know the name of the island and he also did not know where it was.

But they can swim very well, Olon said.

Yes, he had once heard of an island where the people could swim very well.

Show him the map, Olon said.

I got the map and showed it to the old man.

Is this the island?, Olon asked, and he pointed to one of the larger islands.

Yes, maybe that's it.

We'll find it, Olon said.

After twelve days we had only one more island left. It was a small island and not very many people lived there. We cast anchor in the evening, and when we heard music come out of the dark and saw lights moving, Olon and I took the dinghy from the Arimassa and rowed ashore. There was a party in front of the house of the chief. His son had been married that day and they were celebrating a big wedding.

People came out to meet us, laughing and singing, and we were invited inside. There were a lot of guests. Nearly all the inhabitants of the island had come to the celebration.

Olon asked: Are there also swimmers here?

Oh yes, they already knew about us. A boat had come with guests from another island and they had told them everything about us.

No, there were no swimmers here.

But there has to be an island somewhere, where swimmers live, Olon said.

Certainly, there surely must be such an island somewhere.

But we have searched all the islands already, I said.

Well, that makes it more difficult.

Have you ever heard stories about it?, Olon asked.

Oh yes, they would take us to an old man, he knew some stories.

The old man told us of a small island, where only two men lived, a father and a son. They were poor and they were fishermen. And they were very sad, because the father had no grandchild, because the son had no wife. Only the two of them lived on the small island and every day they went out fishing.

With nets, Olon said.

Yes, with nets.

And they swam to bring up the nets, Olon said.

Well, yes, they swam and one fine day they caught something heavy in their nets, and when they hauled it up, a beautiful woman was in it. The son married the beautiful woman, and on the evening of their wedding the son had to promise her that he would never ask her where she came from. And they had two children, a son and a daughter, and the wife stayed as beautiful as on the first day. But when the son was eighteen years old, he asked his father where his mother had come from, and the father did not want to say that he had fished up his wife out of the sea with a net and he asked his wife: Where do you come from?

And his wife said: I am the daughter of the king of the big island in the south, where the day is longer than the night and the night warmer than the day.

And where all good swimmers live, Olon said.

Yes, where all good swimmers live. And when she said that, she disappeared. And no one ever saw her again.

The next day we sailed south with the Hecuba. We had sent Mrs. Olon home with the Arimassa. We had a good eastern wind and the Hecuba was a smooth sailer. Olon had charted a course and we relieved each other at the rudder. When it became afternoon on this first day of sailing, I said: Olon, buddy, we know what we are doing, don't we? We are approaching a sea with a ship full of food, beer, and rum, a sea so wide we can't even begin to imagine. A sea without islands. There are no more islands there in the south, everyone knows that. We are approaching an empty sea, and if we would want to see land, we would have to turn around. Do you really know what it means when you have to turn around after having sailed for seven days without seeing land? I don't think you are a man to turn around. You would continue sailing.

Olon said: Don't you worry about a thing. I know for sure that the island exists. A lot of things came back to me last night. I'm beginning to remember certain things.

Have you been there before?, I asked.

I must have been there, Olon said. I have been on so many islands in my life. But I'm beginning to remember it better and better. It is a low oblong island. The highest point is not more than thirty, forty feet or so. From west to east it isn't any longer than thirty miles and it is perhaps five miles wide.

Well, well, I said, all of a sudden you certainly have quite a lot to tell about the island.

Some more will probably come back to me, Olon said. I am beginning to remember things now.

In the evening he came and stood next to me at the rudder.

There are two large villages on the island, he said. One of them they built on the eastern tip, and the other one is twenty miles further west. I don't know yet which village would be best to head for.

I would head for the village in which the King lives, I said.

The King?, Olon asked.

The King with the beautiful daughter, I said. The daughter who never grows old.

Drop dead, Olon said. He walked away from the rudder. I saw him lean against the cabin. He looked up at the stars. A little later he came back again.

Give me the rudder, he said. I'll stay on deck tonight. I have to keep an eye on the course. I believe there is a strong current here from west to east. We have to be careful that we don't drift easterly.

At sunrise I relieved Olon. He went to the cabin and at ten he came back again.

We are sailing to the eastern village, he said. I remember now. There is a small harbor there, and at the tip of the island is a light. It isn't much, the light. Just a large dish, actually, which they fill with oil every night and put a burning wick inside it. But the harbor is excellent. A small bay with a pier. And most of the fishermen live in the eastern village, too. We will head for the eastern village. But I don't trust this current here. I'm afraid that we drifted too far east last night, and you, of course, managed to foul up the course this morning.

I didn't take my eyes off the compass, I said. That wasn't true. I had been looking at the sea this morning. I had been looking out over the wide empty sea for the low island with the two villages. But all the while I had kept on the southern course as well as possible.

I'm thinking about the possibility of living there perhaps, Olon said. Those swimmers might not even want to leave their island. I really shouldn't have sent Mrs. Olon and the Arimassa home. I came up with some plans last night. I could have small cargo ships built and load them every month, or every week if need be, with fish and have the Arimassa drag them to the biggest storage place they have around here. And I'd have a shed built on the eastern tip behind the light. I have to be able to store fish, of course. And I've got to have salt. I am going to live in the other village. Or maybe in between the two villages. Yes, that would even be better. Let them know that you are still a little different from them. The people themselves appreciate that sort of thing, too.

I wouldn't mind that myself, I said.

Of course, Olon said, of course you can join me. You could manage the preserving process.

Is it a beautiful island?, I asked.

Oh, Olon said, beautiful, beautiful. It has quite a lot of vegetation. A lot of small hedges to separate the plots of the farmers. The farmers live in the west.

I wouldn't mind having a small farm there, I said.

Sure, Olon said, sure, why not.

That night I kept watch from midnight until sunrise. I looked at the stars, I looked at the compass, and I peered to the south, looking for the dish with burning oil which should finally be rising up out of the waves.

According to Olon, we had drifted far too much east again, and he said he would stay on deck from now on until we had the island in sight. When I came back up toward the evening, I noticed that our course was almost west-southwest. The wind had become much stronger and we were making good time.

I remember now what the island is called, Olon said. It is called Raas. I also have a feeling we will get there by tonight. I am going to go to sleep for a few hours. Call me if you see anything, and call me at two o'clock in any case. And keep her on this course.

It was soon completely dark. The wind decreased somewhat at eight o'clock, and at twelve o'clock it increased slightly. At one o'clock I thought: I'm going to call Olon because it is becoming a little bit too rough for me. I was sitting at the rudder, and I stood up to make myself better heard. And at that moment I saw the light. A moment later it was gone again, the sea was rough. But I had seen the light. I yelled: Olon! Olon!

It took a good five minutes before I managed to wake him up.

It sure takes you long enough, I said.

What's the matter?, he asked.

The island, I said. The light of the island.

Where?, Olon asked.

I pointed in the direction where I had seen the light. A little later it was there again. Olon saw it too.

We have drifted even further off than I had thought, Olon said. He took the rudder. I noticed that the course became west-northwest.

Can you feel we are entering the lee of the island?, Olon called out. I nodded, but I did not look at him. The light I had seen first no longer disappeared in the waves. There was another light and then another. I went to the cabin. I knew that if we wanted to, we could go ashore in our own harbor in half an hour. We had taken the shortest route home with the Hecuba, to our last island.

Olon was standing at the rudder. He wanted to go in with daylight. The wind was strong. He wanted to keep on sailing around until sunrise. I would give him until sunrise.

The Unknown Island
A Stranger Narrates

WE felt that we had made a sudden sharp turn, and when Clarence came crawling toward us, we realized something was wrong. Clarence shouted something, but not until he was lying right next to me was I able to understand him.

The machine guns are jammed, Clarence shouted. He was as white as a sheet, which was not like him, and when I took a closer look, I saw blood oozing out of his left sleeve. A bullet had gone through the upper part of his arm. Clarence lay down on his side, with his wounded arm up, and I applied a makeshift bandage. Clarence yelled: John has flown into a cloud, and I nodded and saw that Clarence had fainted.

About an hour or so later, we finally made another definite turn, and Ducky began to shout immediately. He was lying on his stomach, looking through the small window and yelling and waving at us. I lay down next to him and pushed him away from the window. Down below I saw a shimmering sea and in that sea a little round green island with a wide white ring around it. We were coming down fast now. The island disappeared, and when I saw it again, we were already directly above it. It was a small island with palm trees and a wide beach, and it was clear that John was going to land on it, for whatever reason.

An awful crash. We were tossed around and on top of each other, and afterwards we lay still. Dead still.

The six of us were standing in the loose sand. John, Spike, David,

Louie, Ducky, and I, and Clarence was lying next to us. He lay down on the ground as soon as possible. We looked around.

The beach was about a hundred feet wide. John had made a beautiful landing. If the coral hadn't smashed the landing gear and if the beach had been firm instead of soft, and if there had been fuel on the island, we would have been able to leave again.

You made a beautiful landing, John, I said.

You made a beautiful landing, John, Louie and David said.

I didn't know it was coral. I didn't know it was that damned coral, John said.

It was a good landing, John, we said.

And here comes the reception committee, Louie said.

I heard confused shouting, and I saw a group of men slowly head in our direction out from under the palms on the beach.

Let's go meet them, John said. Clarence has to be moved out of the sun.

We went to meet them. When we were right in front of them, we raised our right hands to greet them, and we said: Hello! Those opposite us also made some gesture or another and some of them even tried to salute, but not one of them said a word.

John stepped forward and said, pointing behind him: We have had an accident.

The men did not say anything.

John said: Accident, do you understand? Ac-ci-dent. Kaput. All kaput!

The men grinned and said something to each other.

John asked again: What's this place called? Name of this island? Name! And meanwhile he stamped on the ground with his foot.

Be careful, Louie said, or you'll bang their empire right down into the water.

But the men did not say a word.

They don't understand us, John said. What should we do?

We certainly must do something, but what?

We will walk around the island, John said. Not that it will get us anywhere, because as far as I know from what I saw from above, we are abandoned by God and man alike, but we will give it a try.

We have to have water, Spike said. Water to drink and water to clean Clarence's wound. Water! he suddenly shouted in the direction of the men. Wa-ter! Wa-ter-to-drink!

The men grinned. A few of them walked away.

They have understood, Spike said optimistically.

But those that walked away remained standing with another group.

They talked to each other and pointed at us, and then the others also broke out in a grin.

Let me try, Louie said. He stood in front of one of the men. He made a cup with his hands and drank. He drank as convincingly as anyone I have ever seen do it in reality. His Adam's apple moved up and down as though a billiard ball was going down his throat. The men watched Louie with interest. One of them involuntarily wiped the side of his mouth with a hand. Louie pointed at that man and then pointed at himself and nodded at him a few times. The man laughed and nodded in return and shouted a few loud sharp sounds. We saw a couple of small boys run inland, and after a few minutes they came back with a can. A can filled with water. It was spilling over on all sides, but it was water. The boys put the can down in front of the man who had shouted, and the man pointed at the can, looked at Louie, and laughed triumphantly. Louie walked up to the man and gave him a cigarette. The man laughed again and showed the cigarette to the other men.

The water was dirty. It was damned dirty. It stank. We have to boil the water, Louie said. And we should find out where they get the water from. It stinks, of course, because the can stinks. Leave it to me.

We finally decided to leave it to Louie. Louie would stay with Clarence, along with Ducky and Spike, and take everything from the plane that we could still use, and seek closer contact with the men. John, David, and I would walk around the island.

Wouldn't it be better if we cut right across it?, David asked. Of course that was better, and we were on our way. Immediately a small group of men separated from the others and followed us at a distance. We first came to some kind of village of straw huts. A few women scurried away as we approached and disappeared into the huts. When we looked behind us, we saw their heads sticking out of the houses. Outside the village there was a path leading in a northern direction. We followed the path, which slowly ascended. The small group of men kept following us. After three quarters of an hour we reached the top of a hill, and we were able to look over the whole island on all sides. And we saw nothing but sea.

Well, at least we know now, John said. Let's head back, boys.

Louie was sitting by a fire, on which the can of water was boiling. He was busy plucking a chicken.

Louie had wanted to get some eggs, the others told us. Louie had crouched down in a squatting position, had pulled an anxious face, had flapped with his arms, and had then walked away cackling. The man who had understood him earlier laughed again and called out something. A bit later they heard a violent cackling, and then a chicken was put down in front of Louie. Louie gave the man a dollar.

That's fine too, Louie said. Chicken soup, boys, Chicken soup, Clarence!

Clarence had come around a bit and was lying comfortably in the shade of the palms. But Spike did not want to leave it at that. He grabbed the chicken out of Louie's hands, went over to the man, pointed at himself, and said with emphasis: Name Spike! He then pointed at the chicken and asked: Name what?

The men laughed again and shouted something. A bit later we heard an awful racket, and they brought a second chicken.

You have to give that man a dollar, Spike, Louie said.

Spike sighed and gave the man a dollar.

We've got to get out of here, boys, John said.

That quieted us all down.

We had to get out. Of course we had to get out. We did not know where we were, but we had to get out of the place. How? Did ships call here? Did ships leave from here? There were a couple of tubs lying on the beach. Half-shells, that's the shape they had. And they probably sail in those things around here. Where did they sail to? How would we ask them that?

Suddenly Spike jumped up. I got it!, he shouted. He stood in front of Louie's friend, pointed at himself, and said: Name Spike! Then he pointed at one of the little boats and asked with emphasis: Name what? and in the meantime he waved a few dollars in front of the man. The man laughed and shouted something to the others. They all started to laugh, and some of them shouted something back. Then the man said something to Spike, and Spike repeated his gestures. Nothing happened.

In the meantime, John had spread out his flight map. He called to one of the men and pointed at his map. A few men came closer and looked with interest. They did not laugh this time.

Where are we, John?, we asked.

John shrugged his shoulders. Here somewhere, he said, and he circled a fairly large area on the map with his forefinger. One of the men bent over the map. Don't say anything, John whispered. Don't do anything.

The man beckoned one of the other men, and he too bent over the map. They said something to each other, and they shouted something to the others. And then they all began to laugh in unison.

They're saying that it's a lousy map, Louie said. A lousy map because their island isn't on it.

We have to make a plan, David said.

Drop dead, John said. What do you think we are doing.

Louie had cut the chicken in pieces and threw the pieces in the boiling water.

Do you feel like a bowl of soup, Clarence?, he shouted. Boys, there are coconut shells all over the beach. Go get some and clean them, then we can use them for the soup.

We collected some of the better shells, and we cleaned them in a new can of water that Louie had them bring. When Louie said that the soup was ready, we sat down. The men started to trickle away.

After dinner we stayed put, lying down on the ground rather listlessly. Spike was the only one still nosing around. He didn't give up. From time to time we could hear him shout: Name Spike! Name what?

Louie, John said. Why don't you see if you can find us a place to stay. Louie stood up readily and walked to the village. He came back half an hour later.

I have rented a small but splendid little villa for you, he said. Well furnished, with wide couches and two chairs, one without a seat. In addition there are two pillows for Clarence. A little greasy, but what the hell.

We got up and followed Louie. He took us to a small hut that totally lacked a front wall. There were indeed a few benches on which at least four men could lie next to each other. We took everything we had to the hut. We installed ourselves. We lay down.

What on earth is that screeching?, Ducky asked the following morning.

Birds, David said. We looked up.

Parrots!, Louie shouted. White parrots.

Spike walked up to a man. There still were men watching us. Spike said: Name Spike! Name what? and he pointed at the parrot.

Spike, cut that out, damn it, Ducky said.

Come on, boys, it's nice out, David said.

Louie imitated a chicken. The man brought a chicken. I will get the water myself, Louie said. There are all kinds of wells around here.

What should we do, John said. What are we going to do, for God's sake.

Then I said something. I said: Louie should go over to one of those boats and try to make it clear that we want to leave this place. But nothing came of it. Louie came back half an hour later. He said that the men were probably able to understand but that they just did not want to or dare to.

John pulled out his map. One of the men came closer. John pointed on the map in a southern direction, pointed at the man, pointed at the boat, pointed at all of us. The man did not grin. He looked helpless. We all looked helpless.

We have to go to one of the larger islands, I said. An island where they have a telephone so we can call our base. There are such islands around here.

Just tell them that, Spike, Louie said. And he walked up to a man himself and imitated a telephone. Rrrring, rrring, rrring. The man laughed.

We slept uncomfortably that night. Clarence had a fever and asked several times for water. We were all happy when it became light again. Louie walked to the village and returned with ten eggs. A chicken had laid an egg, right by his feet. He had picked it up, gone inside a house, and there had held up all ten fingers.

But our mood soured again after breakfast. Spike walked away.

We saw him nosing around the houses of the village, and we heard him shout from time to time: Name Spike! Name what? The others remained lying listlessly under our little sloping roof.

We have to leave this place, boys, John said.

We've got to find an island with a telephone, I said.

We will be having chicken soup again, boys, Louie said.

In the afternoon, when no one was looking, I walked over to one of the men. I stood in front of him and imitated a telephone conversation. I dialed a number, I picked up the receiver and held a short conversation. The man started to grin shyly and walked away.

The next day Clarence's arm was red-hot. John said that Louie had to go to the village with the map. You show them the big island, with our base, John said. They've got to understand some time. Louie walked away. I decided that I'd try telephoning again near a few of the men. The men kept on grinning. From time to time I heard Spike shout: Name Spike! Name what? Louie returned from the village empty-handed.

On the fifth day Clarence's arm began to turn green. Spike was now on the side of the men and grinned along with them, whenever we did something to make the men grin. On the sixth day I stood near the largest of the boats. Two young men were working on it. And in that moment I thought of my grandfather and of the telephone that my grandfather had had. An old-fashioned wooden box with a crank and a horn to speak in up front. The men were doing something to the boat's rigging. I picked up the handle of my grandfather's telephone and began to crank it. The men watched me thoughtfully. I was put through. I started to yell hello.

Then one of the men said very clearly: Tilpun.

Tilpun, I said softly. I shouted: Tilpun! I screamed: Tilpun!! I ran across the beach to the hut: Tilpun!! Tilpun!! Tilpun!!

Calm down, John said. What's the matter?

I took a deep breath. I said: Telephone is tilpun. They understood it right away. Come with me, John said. Louie, you too.

We all went with him. We came to the boat. Louie pointed at the boat, at the men, at us. He pointed in the distance, and he said: Tilpun. The men nodded. Louie took some dollars out of his pocket. We all took dollars out of our pockets. The men nodded again.

That same afternoon I was at sea with the two men. They had wanted to take only one of us along. John had pointed at me. Because I knew the language, Louie had said. The island was far behind me already, but toward evening there was still no land in sight in the other direction.

A kind of little house had been built on the ship, but it was so low that I could only either sit or lie in it. I actually slept quite a bit. When I came out the next morning, there was still no land in sight. The wind was faint, and I think that the boat was practically motionless. The men gave me some food. I ate, I sat on top of the little house, or I slept in the little house. And the day passed. I asked: Tilpun?, and I pointed in front of me. Tilpun?, I asked, and I made a sweeping gesture with my arm as if to imitate the path of the sun. Tilpun?

The men nodded patiently. Tilpun, they said, and they also pointed in front of them.

I asked: Tilpun?, and I waved with my arm again.

The men started to laugh. And suddenly I began to laugh myself. I howled with laughter. I wanted to hang over the railing and laugh and laugh. One of the men grabbed me, just as I was about to fall overboard. I said: Oh yes, of course, there is no railing. Kind men. Friendly men. I thanked them: Tilpun, I said. And I started laughing again. They put me in the small house. I lay on the wooded floor shaking with laughter.

The next morning they opened the door. We were in a bay moored to a pier. On shore were small houses. Small stone houses. The men pointed at them and said: Tilpun. I stepped onto the little pier. One of the men walked in front of me. He went inside a small white house and spoke to a man sitting behind a desk. The man behind the desk stood up and went to the corner of the room. And I saw that a wooden telephone was hanging on the wall. A telephone with a crank and a horn. The man cranked, and a moment later he spoke into a horn. He beckoned me. He put the receiver in my hand. I said: Tilpun! in the receiver. I heard a voice at the other end. I said: I am an American pilot. Can you understand me? The voice at the other end said: Yes, I understand you very well. What can I do for you?

I did not say anything. I clasped my hand around the receiver, and I used the other to stroke my cheek with the horn. And I cried like a man.[1]

Half an hour later our base was informed, and three hours later two hydroplanes landed at the unknown island, the name of which I still hear sometimes when I lie awake at night: a name like the screeching of a white parrot.

Beyond the Horizon

Last night was the final night on board, and I dreamed about the islands. I have left the islands and I will probably never go back. Today, this afternoon even, I will be back in the country of my birth, the country I left back then to go live on the islands.

The last evening on board is always celebrated. I celebrated it by drinking rum in the lounge with my roommate from nine until midnight. At the end of those three hours, he must undoubtedly have been the doctor of the islands to me, and the smoking lounge the front room of the doctor's house, and the rum the doctor's rum. I'm sure I also called my roommate doctor. We went back to our cabin at midnight and I fell asleep like a log, of course, and then, for the first time since the trip began, I dreamed of the islands. I was still talking to Mr. Zeinal, when I woke up a little while ago. Woke up early. Everyone on board woke up early this morning, because the coastline would be in sight at seven o'clock, the coastline of the country where I came from and where I will live from now on.

When I get on deck, everyone is standing at the railing on starboard. I squeeze in between two passengers and I see the coastline. I hear the people shout all kinds of things, they probably recognize certain points, and the passenger on my left tells me: We'll be there in about three hours, and I think: I couldn't care less whether or not we are there in three hours. As far as I am concerned, we can keep right on going, farther north. But with an empty ship. An empty ship on an empty sea, and a little later I say to my neighbor on my right: We'll be there in about three hours.

And indeed we do arrive in three hours. We sail down a canal to a big harbor. There are bicycles and cars along the canal. The people on them or in them are people who have stayed here. They did not go to the islands. They stayed in this country and have become strangers to us now. To us. To all the people on this ship. And we have become strangers to them, and that seems to bring us, the passengers, in the end, closer together. The voyage lasted four weeks, and I am not the only one who longs to stay behind on an empty ship and continue sailing on alone. We have seen too much of each other. We have exchanged too many confidences. But I'm now standing at the railing with another passenger, and we both see the bicycles and the cars, and I lean toward him, toward my fellow inhabitant of the islands, and I say: Well . . . here we are again, and he nods and he says: Yes.

I go to my cabin to open and close my suitcase one more time, and on the way I meet the head servant of our ship. Almost all the servants on our ship were born and raised on the islands, and I knew this one's native village. I even visited it regularly to supervise the tax collection and to imprison people and to inspect the crops. The head servant in turn knew Mr. Zeinal, but then Mr. Zeinal was a famous person on our island. The only thing the head servant did not believe was that Mr. Zeinal had magic powers. He had seen too much of the world to believe that, and too little to start believing again.

I want to speak to him. I want to say something about the island and about the village he comes from, but he walks on, he doesn't have time. I gave him his tip yesterday and now he doesn't have time anymore. He probably does not feel at all like listening to more sentimental talk about the hole where he lived as a child. He will never return to his village in order to stay there. Surely he has a wife and children in the large seaport where we will arrive in a few hours.

We are moored in the large port, and from now on things happen slowly and inevitably. We slowly walk along the decks, and from time to time we put down our suitcases on it. We slowly go down the gangway and across the wharf to a shed where we have to wait a long time. And then, when all is done that needs to be done and we are finally standing outside the shed, everything starts moving very quickly. Then we are no longer we. Then there are no passengers, no fellow travelers from the islands any more. Then there is only me. Me alone in a taxi, me alone in a café behind a cup of coffee. Me alone, giving a waiter too large a tip. Me alone in a train, taking me away, away from the ship, away from the sea, away from the islands.

A day later.
There is a garden in back where I live and there is no garden in front. In the islands there always were gardens in front. I cannot remember ever going to the back of my house in the islands. No one else ever did, either. Everyone always sat in front of the house in the evening, in a chair near a lamp, at a table with something to drink on it. At Mr. Zeinal's it was coffee, and at the harbor master's it was gin, and at the doctor's it was rum. Taronggi III always had his guests' preferred drink standing on the table.

But here I leave the front door and I am on the street. At four o'clock in the afternoon I am on the street with people who walk past me and scrutinize me from aside because they know only too well that I have come from the islands. Then those people go home, or wherever, and say to their family: Another one back from the islands, and the family says: It must be one from so and so, and meanwhile I continue walking, and I end up in the café at five o'clock, and the man behind the counter says after the second gin: You must be one from so and so, and I say: Yes, and I say: I'm from the islands. Yes, the man behind the counter had thought so already, and what was it like there in the islands, and I say: Yes, and a little later I say: No, because for a moment I had thought about telling him about Taronggi III, but I don't think I can do it. And so I say a little later: Oh, it was all right, and a little later I get up and pay and go back to the house with the front door.

A day later.
I took the train back to the big seaport today. I have to take care of some final business with the company of the ship that brought me from the islands. It looks, therefore, as if I am making the return trip. The first part of the return trip. All I would have to do at the office of the shipping company is to say: I would like to book passage on the next ship to the islands.

Well sir, they'd say, that's a coincidence! We have one leaving this very afternoon, and a cabin has become available at the last moment. If you make sure to be on board at two o'clock, you can have it.

I arrive at the company office and say: There is still luggage in storage for me. I didn't have an address for it at the time. I do now. Here it is.

They say: We will forward your luggage right away, and I say: Thank you, and I go outside again and I am in the street again and I walk around and at eleven I go to a café and at half past twelve I have my lunch there.

At half past one I am back on the street again. If I were in the islands now, I would go to bed. I would read and doze off until four o'clock. I would get up, have some tea, and go to the doctor or to the club. Or I could think up some excuse to see Mr. Zeinal or Taronggi III, because you don't just stop by at their places.

But it is one thirty now in this city, and I might as well go to the station to catch a train, and then I'll be at five o'clock in the same café I was in on the second day. At least they know me there by now, and that is a pleasant thought, after all. And I enter it rather hastily, and the man behind the counter says: Here is the man from the islands.

There are two other people at the bar, and one of the two says: You're from the islands, you say? I say: Yes, and he says: What's it like there, anyway? I say again that it's all right there, but he insists. Apparently he wants to hear particulars, and I realize that I will probably have to end up telling a bit more. I certainly should be able to tell more about the islands. If only I knew how?

I begin by ordering gin for the four of us, and the man who had questioned me says, pointing at the four glasses: You people knew what to do with this stuff over there, I believe. I say: Yes, pretty much so, and he asks if it's really true that there is a lot of drinking in the islands, and I say: Oh, it depends on what you call a lot. Well, that question is not easily answered, and while we discuss it, the islands fade into the background.

A week later.
I have received a letter from the doctor. The harbor master has been transferred to another island. The harbor master had a fight with my boss, and my boss said: Either that guy leaves or I do.

And then the harbor master left, of course. The doctor had poured some rum, at the end of the letter. And next to it was written rather shakily and messily: Can you still smell it? But I couldn't.

A month later.
I have a new job now. I go to an office every day. My new boss was in the islands at one time. He says: So, you've been there too? I bet you are mighty glad to be back again, aren't you?

I say: Oh.

He says: Here, in this country, in this part of the world, things happen, at least. People really know how to live here. Over there they do the living for you.

I say: True, nothing much happened there. I had just received a letter from the doctor again, this time without rum. I found out that my boss has been transferred. Naturally, this kept my boss's island in an uproar for a week.

I say to my present boss: Once in a while something would happen. Occasionally, you were transferred.

From one hole to the next, says my present boss.

A month later.
I dreamed about the islands again last night, but it was a strange dream. It was not a pleasant dream. I was driving in my car along the northern coast of our main island. I recognized everything. I recognized the houses, but there were no people. All the houses had big signs in their front yards, and on every sign was written in big letters: Transferred.

Notes

Introduction

1 References to the original text in this introduction are to: A. Alberts, *De eilanden* (1952; reprint ed., Amsterdam: Van Oorschot, 1965). Auden's definition of a symbol in W. H. Auden, *The Enchafèd Flood. Three Critical Essays on the Romantic Spirit* (1950; reprint ed., New York: Random House, Vintage Books, 1967), p. 62.

2 Alberts's comments on telling stories in the Indies, in an interview in *NRC Handelsblad*, 15 August 1975.

3 Fairy-tale prince in A. Alberts, *In en uit het paradijs getild* (Amsterdam: Van Oorschot, 1975), pp. 27–28. Hereafter referred to as *Paradijs*.

4 For the islands in Alberts's district see *Paradijs*, pp. 37–41; H. Blink, *Nederlandsch Oost-en-West Indië geographisch, ethnographisch en economisch beschreven*, 2 vols. (Leiden: Brill, 1907), 1:169–77; *Encyclopaedie van Nederlandsch-Indië* under the headings "Kangean-archipel," "Sapudi-archipel," and the names of the individual islands.

5 Kangean and Salambu mentioned in *Paradijs*, pp. 50–51.

6 The description of Ketapang from *Paradijs*, pp. 54–55.

7 The description of Raäs in *Paradijs*, p. 38.

8 Melville's comment about Queequeg's island is echoed by Lewis Carroll's poem, "The Hunting of the Snark," when the Bellman in "Fit the Second" presents a blank map to the crew:

"What's the good of Mercator's North Poles and Equators,
Tropics, Zones, and Meridian Lines?"
So the Bellman would cry: and the crew would reply,
"They are merely conventional signs!

"Other maps are such shapes, with their islands and capes!
But we've got our brave Captain to thank"
(So the crew would protest) "that he's bought *us* the best—
A perfect and absolute blank!"

Martin Gardner, ed., *The Annotated Snark* (New York: Bramhall House, 1962), pp. 47–48. Alberts would very much agree with this sentiment.

9   Atlantis as a legendary realm which, by definition, is presumed to be better than anything at the present. I am only referring to Plato's original creation in the *Timaeus* and the *Critias,* where Critias tells Socrates about Atlantis the way he heard it from Solon. The metaphor of the East Indies as a realm similar to Atlantis becomes even more interesting if one accepts the theory that the vast Malay archipelago represents the lost continent of the Pacific; compare A. Cabaton, *Java, Sumatra, and The Other Islands of the Dutch East Indies* (New York: Scribner's, 1911), pp. 1–3.

10 The European longing for an eastern shore in *Haast hebben in september* (Amsterdam: Van Oorschot, 1975), p. 103.

11 *Nesomanic* is a term used by John Fowles in *Islands* (Boston: Little, Brown, 1978), p. 17. The noun "nesomane" and my adjective here derive from the Greek *nêsos;* Liddell and Scott suggest the marvelous derivation that the noun might come from the Greek verb *neô,* which means "to swim," i.e., as they suggest, as if a person were "floating land."

12 Cape Blanco description in *Paradijs,* p. 11.

13 Fowles's quote from *Islands,* p. 28.

14 Quote about Captain Wietze from A. Alberts, *De honden jagen niet meer* (Amsterdam: Van Oorschot, 1979), p. 81.

15 Quote about a mariner's life from *Honden,* p. 79. Captain Wietze's attempt to hide from ships and the sea in Brazil reminds one of Conrad's characters, especially Jim. Many of Conrad's characters are as much "isolatoes" as Alberts's or Melville's.

16 Auden's comment on the sea in *The Enchafèd Flood,* p. 17.

17 Quote about the sea by Peru from *Haast hebben in september,* p. 104.

18 Quote about the sea by Peru from ibid., p. 110.

19 Alberts's comment on nostalgia from interview in *Algemeen Dagblad,* 15 February 1964. I translated "heimwee" as "nostalgia," although the Dutch word is chiefly used to indicate homesickness. But Alberts connotes more with the word than just that, as is evident from his text "De herfst van het heimwee" in *Haast hebben in september,* pp. 61–70; see below. For that matter, our English term still contains its original Greek meaning of homesickness: *nostos,* which means "returning home," and *algos,* which means "pain."

20 Aart Duclos. I am convinced that most names in Alberts's fiction have a meaning. Alberts shows in the title story of *Haast hebben in september* that he is aware of such meanings. The main character, Madame de Chevreuse, puns on the name of a man she meets. The man's name is Malbâti, and she asks if he is "ill-made" (p. 46). Aart's last name has echoes of the French word *clos,* which can mean closed, shut, completed, and also an enclosure or a field. Aart certainly is "of the fields," and although he is a closed book to most people, he is nevertheless quite secure within his own self.

In "Green," similar vocabulary is used to describe the men the narrator takes along on his first trip. He also speaks of a "retinue" and a "train" of bearers because he too is, after all, a "prince from [a] distant court . . . surrounded by the wall and moat of distinction" (*Eilanden*, p. 17).

21 Quotes about Aart's nobility from A. Alberts, *De bomen* (1953; reprint ed., Amsterdam: Van Oorschot, 1975), p. 105.

22 Both quotes about the might of a forest and the autumnal forest from *Bomen*, p. 61 and p. 70. I have tried to keep the particular rhythm of Alberts's sentence.

The Mexican poet Octavio Paz perceives a similar power in trees. "The trees twist, bend, straighten up again with a deafening creak and strain upward as though struggling to uproot themselves and flee. No, they do not give in. The pain of roots and broken limbs, the fierce stubbornness of plants, no less powerful than that of animals and men. If these trees were suddenly to start walking, they would destroy everything in their path." Octavio Paz, *The Monkey Grammarian,* trans. Helen R. Lane (New York: Seaver Books, 1981), p. 5.

23 Quote about the unconcern of trees from *Bomen*, p. 56; Mr. Barre's drawing described on p. 82.

24 Green man from John Fowles, *The Tree* (Boston: Little, Brown, 1980); it has no pagination. Alberts's *De bomen* seems like a fictional counterpart of Fowles's essay.

25 Quote from the phantom king from A. Alberts, *Maar geel en glanzend blijft het goud* (Amsterdam: Van Oorschot, 1981), p. 61.

26 The Stevenson quote from Robert Louis Stevenson, *Vailima Letters,* 2 vols. (New York: Scribner's, 1906), 1:27.

27 North is often the direction of death in Alberts's fiction.

28 The quotes by Fowles are from *The Tree.*

29 The resemblance between the narrator in the Second Java Fort and the final section of "The Hunt" is suggested textually in the original. The "waaidennen" (p. 114), which provide cover for the narrator as a youth, are paralleled by the "rij bomen met lage takken" of the farm. They too provide cover ("afschermen," p. 116), as does the "struiken en lage bomen" by Florines's house, "die ons dekking gaven" (p. 120). The water near the farm makes the narrator gasp for breath (p. 116) as he did while a boar in the "fort" (p. 114), while the water also connects him to Florines, who is first discovered when he is pouring water over himself (p. 121). On p. 118, the narrator, dead-tired from the march, falls down under some shady bushes, something he also did in the "fort" (p. 114). The column of police troops is just as silent (p. 118) as were the "vervolgers" in "de Veluwe" (p. 113). And, finally, the police troops are said to walk in a "lange sliert" (p. 117), and in the "fort" the children are described as "slierden langs de wallen" (p. 113).

30 Among many other sources on the symbolic value of the boar, see Angelo de Gubernatis, *Zoological Mythology,* 2 vols. (New York: Macmillan, 1872), 1:2–16. If one reads Ovid's accounts of the Calydonian boar hunt and the death of Adonis, it is very clear that part of the symbolism is sexual. If the wounds he inflicts are lethal, the boar has invariably emasculated his adversary. That there is something like an Ovidian metamorphosis in this story is made clear by the use of

that term in both its Latin version and its Dutch equivalent: "wezensverander-ing" (*Eilanden*, p. 114).

31 Malay opinion of the wild boar in W. W. Skeat, *Malay Magic* (1900; reprint ed., London: Frank Cass & Co., 1965), pp. 188–89, 272.

32 Ovid's final lines describing Meleager's death are:

crescunt ignisque dolorque
languescuntque iterum; simul est exstinctus uterque,
inque leves abiit paulatim spiritus auras
paulatim cana prunam velante favilla.
Ovid, *The Metamorphoses*, Bk. 8, ll. 522–25.

33 In *De bomen*, Aart's treasure is also in the center of his magic fortress; see pp. 43–44. Mr. Dalem in *The Meeting Room* goes on an odyssey of Amsterdam after he has temporarily lost his mind, only to return to the house where his mis-fortunes started and where he tries to commit suicide by jumping into the water. The novel also has a circular nature in that he returns to a boardroom meeting with the same people in the same building as when the book started.

34 Eliot quote from T. S. Eliot, *The Complete Poems and Plays 1909–1950* (New York: Harcourt, Brace & World, 1971), p. 145.

35 Mariner's families from an interview in *Hervormd Nederland*, 22 March 1980.

36 Indology and his family in the Indies from an interview in *NRC Handelsblad*, 15 August 1975.

37 A. Alberts, *De Franse Slag* (Amsterdam: Van Oorschot, 1963). The pun in the original title is untranslatable; it refers to doing something hastily and therefore sloppily.

38 His dissertation: A. Alberts, *Baud en Thorbecke, 1847–1851*, vol. 18 of the *Utrechtsche Bijdragen tot de Geschiedenis, het Staatsrecht, en de Economie van Nederlandsch-Indië* (Utrecht: N.V. A. Oosthoek's Uitgevers Maatschappij, 1939), p. 2.

39 Alberts's description of himself from *Paradijs*, p. 28.

40 Many pages have been written on the madness just after the Japanese capitula-tion. One can read Alberts's own sober account of the political aspects in A. Al-berts, *Het einde van een verhouding: Indonesië en Nederland tussen 1945 en 1963* (Alphen aan den Rijn: N. Samson N.V., 1968). Other accounts can be found in more recent, critical works such as: Jan Pluvier, *Indonesië: kolonial-isme, onafhankelijkheid, neo-kolonialisme* (Nijmegen: Socialistiese Uitgeverij, 1978), pp. 58–109; W. F. Wertheim, *Van vorstenrijk tot neo-kolonie* (Amster-dam: Boom, 1978), pp. 118–31; and in English—W. F. Wertheim, *Indonesian Society in Transition* (The Hague: W. van Hoeve Ltd., 1956), pp. 78–87. The British side is represented in a work of fiction: Dirk Bogarde, *A Gentle Occupa-tion* (1980; reprint ed., London: Triad/Granada, 1981).

41 Kina Bureau is described by Alberts in the interview in *NRC Handelsblad*, 15 August 1975.

42 About the unlikely publications of his stories, see a review of Alberts's *De Franse Slag* by R. Nieuwenhuys in *Het Parool*, 28 December 1963.

43 The main character of *The Meeting Room* is a Mr. Dalem. This is also a Java-
    nese word which, particularly in Bali, has mystical overtones. *Dalem* can be
    translated as "within" or "inner." Alberts's novel takes place primarily within
    Mr. Dalem's mind. The term is positive. In Java it stood for a king, or his court, or
    the core of a dynasty, while in Bali it is also part of Balinese dances and theater. In
    Topeng theater, Dalem is a virtuous king, while the Temple of Death in Bali is
    called the Pura Dalem. See Clifford Geertz, *Negara: Theatre-State in Nineteenth
    Century Bali* (Princeton: Princeton University Press, 1980), pp. 58–60; and Ana
    Daniel, *Bali: Behind the Mask* (New York: Alfred A. Knopf, 1981), pp. 71–75.
44 See, for example, *Koning Willem III* (The Hague: Kruseman, 1964).
45 Alberts's latest novel is very difficult to summarize. Let it suffice to say that it
    takes place in Denmark at some unspecified time, in a location that is an island, as
    the sketch in front of the book clearly indicates. The first half deals with the bu-
    reaucracy of this kingdom, especially a minister, a councillor, and the minister's
    niece. Gradually the reader realizes that the story is that of a fourteenth-century
    Danish king, probably Valdemar IV or Valdemar Atterdag, who lived from
    1320 to 1375 and ruled from 1340 to 1375. He was succeeded by his daugh-
    ter Margrete (1353–1412), who ruled as a most formidable queen of Denmark
    from 1376 to 1412. The minister's young niece, called Margrete, resembles the
    medieval queen, while the councillor, Gerner, has certain similarities to the
    queen's councillor, Peder Jensen Lodehat. Gradually the two different eras inter-
    mingle and time flows without demarcation toward a typical Alberts ending, one
    which remains ambiguous.
46 For an interpretation of Alberts's work as autobiography, see the article by Vera
    Illes in *NRC Handelsblad*, 15 August 1975.
47 The final anecdote as told by Alberts from an interview in *Hollands Diep*, 20 De-
    cember 1975. Alberts tells the same story, somewhat differently, in *Per Mailboot
    naar de Oost*, pp. 87–88.

Green

1 "Green" is as much metonymy for the Indies as *The Trees (De Bomen)* was for
   Holland. In fact, Alberts has maintained that the viridity of the northern country
   evoked the tropical verdure. As he said in an interview, he was jobless after he returned to Holland from the tropics and was living with his mother in Appingedam. "And among those green meadows of Appingedam my first story 'Green'
   came into being via the association with the green of the Indies. It became the best
   known story from *The Islands,* though I personally prefer 'The Swamp.' " Interview in *NRC Handelsblad*, 15 August 1975; the same was mentioned in the interview in *Hollands Diep*, 20 December 1975. In the latter, Alberts also mentions
   that the story was based on a real incident. That incident is related in an interview
   in *Hervormd Nederland*, 22 March 1980, and in more detail in Alberts's article
   "Vaarwel Nieuw-Guinea" in *De Groene Amsterdammer*, 4 August 1962. The
   following is based on the last article.

A young Dutch official requested to be stationed in New Guinea (now Irian Jaya). He wound up in a desolate place, in the midst of a dense jungle *(rimbu)*, with only two Javanese prisoners for company. The two prisoners had each killed somebody and they had been sentenced to twenty-five years of hard labor, but they could exchange that for exile in New Guinea, where they would be working as houseboys for the Dutch official.

The young official nearly went crazy. His closest neighbor, a man who taught religion, lived about sixty miles away. The desperate Dutchman would walk for two days through the jungle in order to visit this man. He would stay there for a day or so and then walk back, which took another two days. Back at his lonely post he would burst out in tears while the two murderers tried to comfort him. After a day or so he would repeat the journey. After six months he was relieved of his post because of a nervous breakdown, and the station itself was eliminated.

2 The Northwood becoming a fairy castle with its entrances hidden by vegetation is never realized in this story. One will find a close parallel in the royal domain and the Second Java Fort in "The Hunt." In "Green" the forest represents the perilous aspects of the unconscious, and the magic castle is never found, while in "The Hunt" it is a refuge. Echoes are also found in the description of the so-called palace in "The Meal," in the earthen castle Aart built in *De bomen*, and the labyrinth in *Maar geel en glanzend blijft het goud*.

3 Rumpelstiltskin is, of course, the kobold in the fairy tale who spun straw into gold for the miller's daughter and who demands her child after she becomes queen. He will only desist if she can guess his name. The queen's messenger sees a little man hopping around a fire in front of his house, singing the rhyme that tells the messenger that his name is Rumpelstiltskin. Legends or fairy tales are not only present in *The Islands*, but they are part of the warp and woof of all of Alberts's fiction. This does not mean that it is easy to comprehend his use of them. In *De bomen*, Aart Duclos connects fairy tales with trees, and in the collection of stories *Haast hebben in september*, the first story is a moving version of Andersen's tale about the emperor's nightingale.

4 Stonehenge and Merlin were related in British legends. Merlin is said to have built Stonehenge on Salisbury Plain as a funereal monument. These legends are reviewed in Gerald S. Hawkins, *Stonehenge Decoded* (New York: Doubleday, 1965), esp. pp. 4–17. The association with death is implied in Alberts's story.

5 The lines of verse are also mysterious in the original. "Swingflower" is in the original "slingerbloem," and "slinger" is translated as "swing" here. Perhaps there is a personal association here for Alberts, because in *De bomen* he mentions a "slingerjongetje" (pp. 6, 16).

6 The unsatisfactory coffin and the macabre though comical attempts to fit Peartree's corpse into it are reminiscent of a scene in *Paradijs*, in which Alberts describes the comical funeral of a Barisan officer, when not the coffin but the grave was of improper size (pp. 89–91).

The King is Dead

1 One of the ways that Mr. Solomon's regal aspects are indicated is the description of him as looking entirely yellow. In the Indies yellow was the color of gold and of royalty, and in some parts of Indonesia people of lower rank were forbidden to wear it.

    The name Solomon means "peaceful" in Hebrew, and that quality is part of this native sergeant-major's personality. He also reminds one of the biblical king's sexual prowess by marrying a young woman when he is already an old man. It is of interest to note that Alberts uses the English spelling of the name; in Dutch it is customarily spelled Salomo or Salomon.

2 Attestation was used to translate "attestatie da vita" in the original. In Dutch this refers to a written declaration that somebody is still alive, used especially for collecting one's pension.

The House of the Grandfather

1 The name Taronggi, and the merchant dynasty by that name, seem to be based on reality. In *Paradijs,* Alberts briefly mentions a Taronggi who was the "richest dealer in kapok" in the Sumenep regency (p. 81). The rest of the Taronggi story he based on an actual mercantile dynasty on Madura, founded by a shipwrecked Dutchman by the name of Dirk van Duyne. The ruby-encrusted statue mentioned in "The Treasure" belonged to the Van Duyne Alberts met; he was Dirk III (*Paradijs,* pp. 71–74). This is a minor example to show that Alberts did not use his own experiences straightforwardly but combined events, incidents, and persons to comply with the demands of art and the imagination. Perhaps he chose the name Taronggi rather than Dirk for his fiction because there is a city in northeastern Spain that echoes that name, and which Alberts used as the birthplace of the first Taronggi. Tarragona is the capital of a Spanish province by the same name. It is both a flourishing seaport and an ancient city. It was one of the earliest Roman strongholds outside Italy and became a target of subsequent military campaigns by the Visigoths, Moors, Spanish, French, and British. It is noted for its architecture, commerce, and wine, and it is also the place where the Chartreuse liqueur was made after the monks of the Grande Chartreuse monastery were forced to leave France in the first decade of this century.

The Meal

1 Mr. Zeinal was an Indonesian Alberts knew in Madura (*Paradijs,* pp. 101–7). His real name was Zainal. Like his fictional counterpart, he also had a passion for genealogy. He traced his numerous ancestors to a son of Mohammed and a "giant," and Zainal was far prouder of that giant than of his religious forebear.

2 The detail of the stone coffin and the leaf can also be found in *Paradijs* (pp. 86–87), where a nameless *patih* places a leaf on the sarcophagus of a disreputable ancestor of the prince of Sumenep.

The Hunt

1   Florines may have been modeled after the usurper of the legitimate throne of
    Sumenep. Alberts described him as follows. "He was a young man from the north
    coast [of Madura], a kind of bandit leader who still existed in the twenties of this
    century. According to various descriptions, these leaders were something be-
    tween a Scottish blackmailer and an Italian bandito. They oppressed the popula-
    tion, but did so always in a manner of live and let live" (*Paradijs,* p. 85).

2   The berserk natives who think they are *messiahs* and dress in white is, I think, a
    reference to religious fanatics called *Padris.* The Padris were Islamic zealots who
    fought a holy war (*prang sabil* in Malay and *jihad* in Arabic) in Sumatra in the
    nineteenth century. Originally they were pilgrims *(hadjis)* who had returned
    from Mecca and had formed an orthodox Muslim party. Its members were most-
    ly *tuankus,* or Muslim preachers, better known to us as *mullahs.* They demanded
    the abolition of opium, drinking, gambling, even *sirih*-chewing. Women were
    forced to wear the *chador,* and the men were supposed to wear only white (to
    symbolize moral purity and devotion to Islam) in order to distinguish them from
    the infidel "enemy." Because of the latter practice, they were also called *orang
    putih,* a term widely used by the Malay, which means "white people." They en-
    forced their "laws" with Draconian measures. The Padri movement gained con-
    siderable influence and adherents, and it soon embarked on a campaign of con-
    quest. Anyone resisting their demands was either killed or sold into slavery. In
    the end, the local population had to ask for protection from the Dutch govern-
    ment. The Dutch found it difficult to defeat the Padris. The military campaigns
    lasted from 1821 to 1838 and were fought on both sides with a bitter ferocity.

3   The volunteer militia Florines served in more than likely refers to three actual
    volunteer regiments made up of Madurese. This force, called the Barisan, had its
    own officers but was trained by Dutchmen (*Paradijs,* p. 88).

The Treasure

1   The ruby-studded statue belonged in reality to Dirk van Duyne III. It was a statue
    of Kwan Yin, the Chinese goddess of mercy, about ten inches high, made of gold
    and encrusted with rubies (*Paradijs,* p. 73).

2   Feldspar is the name of a group of minerals that occur in crystalline form. Most
    often of a white or flesh-red color, they are the most important constituents of ig-
    neous rocks.

3   Nicol, or Nicol's prism, named after William Nicol (1768–1851), is a prism so
    constructed as to transmit only the extraordinary ray of doubly refracted light.

The Last Island

1   Olon. This is one of those names Alberts uses which seems to resonate with po-
    tential meaning. Like most of the names in *The Islands,* it is an unusual one and
    not Dutch. It could be the Latin verb *Nolo,* written backwards, which means

"not to be willing," "not to wish." It could also refer to Solon, minus the initial consonant. This would be Plato's Solon, the sage who told Socrates about Atlantis in the *Timaeus* and the *Critias;* or Herodotus's Solon, who told Croesus not to call a man happy until his death (*Histories,* Bk. 1). And the legend the old man tells of the mermaid and the fisherman could well illustrate that point. The Athenian legislator also wrote verse, and it could be that Olon's odyssey through Alberts's archipelago in search of his elusive island resembles the man from Solon's poem "who roams over the fish-breeding sea in the hope of shipping home some profit, driven by terrible winds, quite careless of his life" (*The Penguin Book of Greek Verse,* ed. Constantine A. Trypanis [Harmondsworth: Penguin Books, 1971], p. 153).

One could even wonder if Olon's name is an anagram of the name of the Polynesian god Lono. The Hawaiians thought that Captain Cook was an incarnation of this white god of peace and prosperity. The Hawaiians thought that he had returned on the ships which they compared to "floating islands with masts like forests"—an image which seems to combine several of Alberts's major symbols (see *The Explorations of Captain James Cook In The Pacific As Told By Selections Of His Own Journale 1768–1779,* ed. A. Grenfell Price [1957; reprint ed., New York: Dover, 1971], p. 253). It so happens that the season of this god was from October to November, Alberts's favorite time of the year. See J. C. Beaglehole, *The Life of Captain James Cook* (Stanford: Stanford University Press, 1974), pp. 657–60.

Finally, *Olon* is also contained in Solomon, the name of the king in the story "The King is Dead."

Unfortunately, the names of the ships do not help, though they are certainly uncommon. Olon's schooner is given the name of the unfortunate queen of Troy, *Hecuba,* or *Hecabe* in Greek. She became Odysseus's prize, and after she was killed by the Greeks, she turned into a ferocious black dog. The tugboat's name, *Arimassa,* is equally mysterious. It might contain the word Samaria (which means "watch tower"), the country of the despised Samaritans, or the Malay word for "gold," *mas.*

The Unknown Island

1   Alberts has stated that the events in "The Unknown Island" were based on fact. In an interview in *Hollands Diep,* 20 December 1975, he said that he was standing near the telephone that one of a group of downed American fliers was using to call his base, and that he heard the man cry.